The lightning should have fallen on Ghalib

The lightning should have fallen on Ghalib

Selected Poems of Ghalib

Translated from the Urdu by
Robert Bly and Sunil Dutta

RUPA

First published by
Rupa Publications India Pvt. Ltd 2001
7/16, Ansari Road, Daryaganj
New Delhi 110002

Sales Centres:

Allahabad Bengaluru Chennai
Hyderabad Jaipur Kathmandu
Kolkata Mumbai

ISBN: 978-81-716-7576-0

Seventh impression 2014

10 9 8 7

Printed at Rekha Printers Pvt Ltd., New Delhi

Contents

The Surprises in Ghalib   1

Part I

My Destiny   14
My Spiritual State   18
The Clay Cup   22
When the Day Comes   26
My Head and My Knees   30
About Limits and Meanings   34
Don't Skimp with me Today   38
Fantasies and Jealousies   42
Questions   46
Some Exaggerations   52

Part II

Waiting for God   60
Near the Zam Zam Well   64
The Road with Thorns   68
The Drop and the River   72
About My Poems   76
Rubbing My Forehead   80
The Candle Flame   84
A Lamp in a Strong Wind   88

When My Letter Writer Gets Frightened   92
Desires Come by the Thousands   96

Part III

Leftovers in the Cup   103
When the Sky Clears   106
The Candle That Has Gone Out   110
Where Are the Other Faces?   114
Not Making a Commotion   118
The Bird Gathering Straws   122
Thanking the Robber   126
The Musky Wine of Heaven   130
Behind the Curtain   134
The Sword Wound   138
Ghalib and His Work   139
Selected Bibliography   147
About the Editors   148

The Surprises in Ghalib

Reading the literal versions of Ghalib that Sunil Dutta and I began working on, it was clear to me that some fresh substance was appearing that I hadn't experienced before. For years, I have been fond of Kabir's delight in God and the soul:

> Inside this clay jug there are canyons and pine mountains,
>   and the maker of canyons and pine mountains!
> All seven oceans are inside, and hundreds of millions
>   of stars...
>
> If you want the truth, I will tell you the truth:
> Friend, listen: the God whom I love is inside.
>
> *(Translated by Robert Bly)*

Rumi is equally sure:

> This moment this love comes to rest in me, many
>   beings in one being.
> In one wheat grain a thousand sheaf stacks.
> Inside the needle's eye a turning night of stars.
>
> *(Translated by Coleman Barks)*

This enthusiasm, this surety, so far beyond the hopes we usually have for change, widens the boundaries of our soul in a way it is not used to, moving it toward ecstasy and joy.

1

It is as though when Kabir writes a letter to God, God always answers. We could say that when Ghalib writes a letter to God, God doesn't answer. Ghalib says:

> When I look out, I see no hope for change.
> I don't see how anything in my life can end well.

Ghalib's lines, so elegant and sparse, stretch the muscles that we use for truth, muscles we rarely use.

> My destiny did not include reunion with my Friend.
> Even if I lived a hundred years, this failure would be
>   the same.

Ghalib's tart, spicy declaration of defeated expectations ranges over many subjects:

> Heart-sorrow eventually kills us, but that's the way
>   heart is.
> If there were no love, life would have done the trick.

This shift from the buoyant confidence of Kabir, Rumi and Mirabai to the disappointment of Ghalib: what could it mean? Perhaps the turn to failure is natural six centuries after Rumi and four centuries after Kabir. Perhaps spiritual achievement involves more difficulty now than it did in the thirteenth century or perhaps this change in tone has nothing to do with history at all. Perhaps Ghalib writes only six letters a day to God, instead of forty; perhaps he's distracted from the Road by the very love affairs that are to him the essence of the Road. He is a truth-teller around losing the Road. Awareness of this change was my first surprise.

Another surprise I felt as we worked lay in discovering that Urdu has no pronouns to distinguish gender. Some of Ghalib's highly flavored and elaborate love poems declare that his lover doesn't answer his letters or is capriciously cruel or generally inaccessible. There is no way of knowing from the "you" or from objective pronouns whether the person he is addressing is a woman or a man. Moreover, one can't tell whether it is a divine or human personage.

A gift given by such pronouns is that the question of whether the divine is male or female is bypassed from the start. We are freed in one stroke from the issue of God's gender which has so bedeviled Western religion.

Moreover, when the word *"you"* can refer to either a divine or a human "you," the description of a love affair taking place on the human plane resonates on the divine plane as well:

Others in your poetry gathering kiss the wine cup;
But we remain thirsty even for the invitation.

Ghalib says in one ghazal:

I'll write this letter even though it may not have a
message.
I'll send it just because I'm a lover of your name.

An Indian friend recently said to me, "At the university I loved Ghalib. I memorized his poems. He described all my experiences in love affairs. Now that I'm older, I read some of the same poems but I now experience them as written to God."

Some of Ghalib's poems are, in essence, pure love poems to a human lover, or so they seem to me; and others are clearly poems to God. But many hold both possibilities in reserve.

My message hasn't received a reply so I guess I'll
write another.
I think I know what the Great One will say anyway

Such a poem seems to beg to be read in two senses simultaneously.

Why shouldn't I scream? I can stop. Perhaps
The Great One notices Ghalib only when he stops screaming.

If it seems clear that the poem is addressed at least partially to God, we have sometimes used the phrase "the Great One" instead of a pronoun such as "he" or "she."

When a poem is clearly addressed to God, we sometimes use the word "You":

Since nothing actually exists except You,
Then why do I keep hearing all this noise?

Our perception of "things" as real doesn't quite fit with the idea that they don't actually exist. One Muslim belief sees the universe we know as a mixture of the Existent and the Non-Existent. Things such as trees, streets, people, and clouds all belong to Non-Existence: they are only shadows thrown by a genuinely existent Sun.

These magnificent women with their beauty astound me.
Their side-glances, their eyebrows, how does all that
    work? What is it?

These palm trees and these tulips, where did they
    come from?
What purpose do they serve? What are clouds and wind?

I think this is a marvelous poem. He ends by saying:

The abundant objects of the world mean nothing at all!
But if the wine is free, how could Ghalib hold back?

This last poem lets us see the amazing way that Ghalib's ghazals are put together. No clear thread unites all the couplets.

For example, if we return to the poem mentioned above, "My Spiritual State," which begins:

> When I look out, I see no hope for change.
> I don't see how anything in my life can end well.

We see a statement of theme. But a fresh theme, a little explosion of humor and sadness, arrives in the next stanza:

> Their funeral date is already decided, but still
> People complain that they can't sleep.

The third couplet, or *sher,* embarks on a third theme:

> When young, my love-disasters made me burst out laughing.
> Now even funny things seem sober to me.

It slowly becomes clear that we are dealing with a way of adventuring one's way through a poem utterly distinct from our habit of textual consistency in theme. Most of the poems we know, whether written in English, French, German, or Hausa, tend to follow from an idea clearly announced at the start. "Something there is that doesn't love a wall." The poet then fulfills the theme, often brilliantly, by drawing on personal experience, and by offering anecdotes, dreams, other voices: "Good fences make good neighbors.' By the end, the theme is fulfilled. The ghazal form does not do that. It invites the reader to discover the hidden center of the poem or the hidden thought that ties it all together, a hidden center unexpressed by the poet himself or herself. I find this delicious. Moreover, when we arrive at the final *sher,* where, according to our typical expectations, the poet should clinch his argument, Ghalib often does exactly the opposite. He confounds everyone by making a personal remark:

> Your talk about spiritual matters is great, Oh Ghalib.
> You could have been thought of as a sage if you
>   didn't drink all the time.

Over the centuries, the ghazal writers have found a way of keeping the mystery of the poem intact, or perhaps it is a way of asking the reader to do more work than Western poets ask. This ghazal way refuses to accommodate our felt need to have the windows lined up, with one beam of light shining straight through them all. In a ghazal, it is as if the writer has thrown a group of handsome bones onto the field, and the reader has to put them together to make a dog, or if he or she prefers, a larger companion, perhaps a horse. This holding of mystery resounds in the poem called "When the Day Comes." It begins:

> One can sigh, but a lifetime is needed to finish it.
> We'll die before we see the tangles in your hair loosened.

The second stanza says:

> There are dangers in waves, in all those crocodiles
>   with their jaws open.
> The drop of water goes through many difficulties
>   before it becomes a pearl.

The third embarks on a different thought:

> Love requires waiting, but desire doesn't want to wait.
> The heart has no patience; it would rather bleed to death.

Later he evokes the delight of the poetry readings usually held in private houses in his time.

> How long is our life? How long does an eyelash flutter?
> The warmth of a poetry gathering is like a single spark.

The last stanza says:

> Oh Ghalib, the sorrows of existence, what can cure
>   them but death?
> There are so many colors in the candle flame, and
>   then the day comes.

I want to take this opportunity to thank Sunil Dutta for the hundreds of hours of labor he has put into these translations. Our work would begin as he wrote out each couplet in Urdu script; a word-by-word version in English, awkward and virtually incomprehensible, followed. Sunil would then abandon the Urdu word order and create two lines in English that hinted at the content of the Urdu. So many ambiguities would be omitted in this version that he usually followed by writing several paragraphs of prose to bring the hidden cultural, religious, or philosophical questions out into the open. At that point I would enter the process and try to compose a couple of lines that would resonate a little with each other. Imposed meanings would stick out here and there like burrs on a dog, and we would have to painstakingly remove those burrs.

Perhaps in the future others will be able to do better with Ghalib's poems than we have done; we know that our versions have flaws. But each of us has drawn on his own, separate delight in Ghalib, and as Ghalib says, "This poem has come to an end, but my longing to praise hasn't."

—Robert Bly

Part I

मेरी क़िस्मत

ये न थी हमारी क़िस्मत के विसाले-यार होता
अगर और जीते रहते, यही इंतज़ार होता

तेरे वादे पे जिये हम, तो ये जान झूट जाना
कि ख़ुशी से मर न जाते, अगर एतबार होता

तेरी नाज़ुकी से जाना, कि बंधा था अहदे बोदा
कभी तू न तोड़ सकता, अगर उस्तुवार होता

कोई मेरे दिल से पूछे तेरे तीरे-नीमकश को
ये ख़लिश कहां से होती, जो जिगर के पार होता

ये कहां कि दोस्ती है, कि बने है दोस्त नासेह
कोई चारासाज़ होता, कोई ग़मगुसार होता

रगे-संग से टपकता वो लहू कि फिर न थमता
जिसे गम समझ रहे हो, ये अगर शरार होता

गम अगरचे जां-गुसिल है, पै कहाँ बचें कि दिल है
ग़मे-इश्क़ ग़र न होता, ग़मे-रोज़गार होता

कहूं किस से ये कि क्या है, शबे-ग़म बुरी बला है
मुझे क्या बुरा था मरना अगर एक बार होता

हुए मर के हम जो रूसवा, हुए क्यों न ग़र्क़े दरिया
न कहीं जनाज़ा उठता, न कहीं मज़ार होता

उसे कौन देख सकता, कि यगाना है वो यकता
जो दुई की बू भी होती, तो कहीं दो-चार होता

ये मसाइले-तसव्वुफ़, ये तेरा बयान 'ग़ालिब'
तुझे हम वली समझते, जो न बादाख़्वार होता

12

یہ نہ تھی ہماری قسمت کہ وصال یار ہوتا

یہ نہ تھی ہماری قسمت کہ وصالِ یار ہوتا'
اگر اور جیتے رہتے' یہی انتظار ہوتا

اگر اور جیتے رہتے' یہی انتظار ہوتا

ترے وعدہ پر جئے ہم' تو یہ جان جھوٹ جانا
کہ خوشی سے مر نہ جاتے' اگر اعتبار ہوتا

تری نازکی سے جانا کہ' بندھا تھا عہد بودا
کبھی تو نہ توڑ سکتا' اگر استوار ہوتا

کوئی میرے دل سے پوچھے' ترے تیر نیم کش کو
یہ خلش کہاں سے ہوتی' جو جگر کے پار ہوتا

یہ کہاں کی دوستی ہے کہ' بنے ہیں دوست ناصح
کوئی چارہ ساز ہوتا' کوئی غم گسار ہوتا

رگِ سنگ سے ٹپکتا' وہ لہو کہ' پھر نہ تھمتا
جسے غم سمجھ رہے ہو' یہ اگر شرار ہوتا

غم اگرچہ جاں گسل ہے' پہ کہاں بچیں کہ دل ہے
غم عشق گر نہ ہوتا' غم روزگار ہوتا

کہوں کس سے میں کہ کیا ہے! شبِ غم بری بلا ہے
مجھے کیا برا تھا مرنا' اگر ایک بار ہوتا

ہوئے مر کے ہم جو رسوا' ہوئے کیوں نہ غرق دریا
نہ کبھی جنازہ اٹھتا' نہ کہیں مزار ہوتا

اسے کون دیکھ سکتا کہ' یگانہ ہے وہ یکتا
جو دوئی کی بو بھی ہوتی' تو کہیں دوچار ہوتا

یہ مسائلِ تصوّف' یہ ترا بیان غالب!

تجھے ہم ولی سمجھتے' جو نہ بادہ خوار ہوتا

13

My Destiny

My destiny did not include reunion with my Friend.
Even if I lived a hundred years, this failure would be the same.

Your promise determined my life; but it was not believable.
If I had believed it, it would have died of joy anyway.

Your hesitation indicates that the thread you tied is weak;
You would never have broken the thread had it been strong.

Ask my heart sometime about your arrow shot from a loose bow.
It would have heart so much if it had actually gone through.

What kind of friendship is this when friends give advice?
I wish they knew healing or simple, ordinary sympathy.

Rocks are hard, so they don't cry, but if your pain
Were genuine, Ghalib, it would make even rocks cry.

Heart-sorrow eventually kills us, but that's the way heart is.
If there were no love, life would have done the trick.

This night of separation, whom can I tell about it?
I think death would be better, because at least it doesn't repeat.

After my death, my reputation worsened. Maybe if I had just
    drowned
In a river, and had no tomb, they would have let Ghalib
    alone.

This great one, who can possibly see her? She is this One.
With just of hint of two, we might have achieved a meeting.

Your talk about spiritual matters is great, Oh Ghalib.
You could have been thought of as a sage if you didn't drink
    all the time

मेरी रूहानी हालत

कोइ उम्मीद बर नहीं आती
कोइ सूरत नजर नहीं आती

मौत का एक दिन मुअय्यन है
नींद क्यों रात भर नहीं आती

आगे आती थी हाले-दिल पे हंसी
अब किसी बात पर नहीं आती

है कुछ ऐसी ही बात कि चुप हूँ
वर्ना क्या बात कर नहीं आती

क्यों न चीखूं कि याद करते हैं
मेरी आवाज गर नहीं आती

हम वहाँ हैं जहां से हमको भी
कुछ हमारी खबर नहीं आती

मरते हैं आरजू में मरने की
मौत आती है पर नहीं आती

काबा किस मुंह से जाओगे 'ग़ालिब'
शर्म तुमको मगर नहीं आती

ثواب طاعت و زہد

کوئی صورت نظر نہیں آتی 　 کوئی امید بر نہیں آتی

نیند کیوں رات بھر نہیں آتی 　 موت کا ایک دن معین ہے

اب کسی بات پر نہیں آتی 　 آگے آتی تھی حال دل پہ ہنسی

ورنہ کیا بات کر نہیں آتی؟ 　 ہے کچھ ایسی ہی بات جو چپ ہوں

میری آواز گر نہیں آتی 　 کیوں نہ چیخوں کہ یاد کرتے ہیں

کچھ ہماری خبر نہیں آتی 　 ہم وہاں ہیں، جہاں سے ہم کو بھی

موت آتی ہے، پر نہیں آتی 　 مرتے ہیں آرزو میں مرنے کی

کعبہ کس منہ سے جاؤگے؟ غالبؔ!

شرم تم کو مگر نہیں آتی!

17

My Spiritual State

When I look out, I see no hope for change.
I don't see how anything in my life can end well.

Their funeral date is already decided, but still
People complain that they can't sleep.

When young, my love-disasters made me burst out laughing.
Now even funny things seem sober to me.

I know the answer-that's what keeps me quiet.
Beyond that it's clear I know how to speak.

Why shouldn't I scream? I can stop. Perhaps
The Great One notices Ghalib only when he stops screaming.

This is the spiritual state I am in:
About myself, there isn't any news.

I do die; the longing for death is so strong it's killing me.
Such a death comes, but the other death doesn't come.

What face will you wear when you visit the Kaaba?
Ghalib, you are shameless even to think of that.

जामे सिफाल

और बाज़ार से ले आयें अगर टूट गया,
साग़रे-जम से मेरा जामे सिफाल अच्छा है

बेतलब दें तो मजा उसमे सिवा मिलता है
वह गदा जिसको न हो खू-ए-सवाल अच्छा है

उनके देखे से जो आ जाती है मुँह पर रौनक,
वह समझते हें कि बीमार का हाल अच्छा है

क़तरा दरिया में मिल जाए तो दरिया हो जाय
काम अच्छा वो जिसका मआल अच्छा है

हमको मालूम है जन्नत की हक़ीक़त लेकिन
दिल के खुश करने को 'ग़ालिब' ये ख्याल अच्छा है

ساغرِ جم سے مرا جامِ سفال اچھا ہے

ساغرِ جم سے مرا جامِ سفال اچھا ہے   اور بازار سے لے آئے، اگر ٹوٹ گیا

وہ گدا، جس کو نہ ہو خوے سوال اچھا ہے   بے طلب دیں، تو مزا اس میں سوا ملتا ہے

وہ سمجھتے ہیں، کہ بیمار کا حال اچھا ہے   ان کے دیکھے سے جو آ جاتی ہے منہ پر رونق

کام اچھا ہے وہ، جس کا کہ مآل اچھا ہے   قطرہ دریا میں جو مل جائے، تو دریا ہو جائے

ہم کو معلوم ہے جنت کی حقیقت، لیکن

دل کے خوش رکھنے کو، غالب یہ خیال اچھا ہے

The Clay Cup

If king Jamshid's diamond cup breaks, that's it.
But my clay cup I can easily replace, so it's better.

The delight of giving is deeper when the gift hasn't been
    demanded.
I like the God-seeker who doesn't make a profession of
    begging.

When I see God, color comes into my cheeks.
God thinks-this is a bad mistake- that I'm in good shape.

When a drop falls in the river, it becomes the river.
When a deed is done well, it becomes the future.

I know that Heaven doesn't exist, but the idea
Is one of Ghalib's favorite fantasies.

सहर होने तक

आह को चाहिये इक उम्र असर होने तक
कौन जीता है तेरी जुल्फ़ के सर होने तक

दाम हर मौज में है हल्क़ा-ए-सदकामे नहंग
देखें क्या गुज़रे है क़तरे पे गुहर होन तक

आशिक़ी सब्र-तलब और तमन्ना बेताब
दिल का क्या रंग करूं खूने-जिगर होने तक

हमने माना कि तग़ाफुल न करोगे, लेकिन
ख़ाक हो जाएंगे हम तुमको ख़बर होने तक

परतवे-खुर से है शबनम को फ़ना की तालीम
मैं भी हूँ इक इनायत की नजर होने तक

यक-नज़र बेश नहीं फुर्सते-हस्ती ग़ाफ़िल
गर्मी-ए-बज़्म है इक रक़्से-शरर होने तक

ग़मे-हस्ती का 'असद' किससे हो जुज़ मर्ग इलाज
शम्अ हर रंग में जलती है सहर होने तक

24

شمع ہر رنگ میں جلتی ہے سحر ہونے تک

آہ کو چاہئے اک عمر' اثر ہونے تک   کون جیتا ہے تری زلف کے سر ہونے تک

دامِ ہر موج میں ہے حلقہ صد کامِ نہنگ   دیکھیں کیا گزرے ہے قطرہ پہ گہرے ہونے تک

عاشقی صبر طلب اور تمنا بے تاب   دل کا کیا رنگ کروں' خونِ جگر ہونے تک

ہم نے مانا کہ' تغافل نہ کروگے' لیکن   خاک ہو جائیں گے ہم' تم کو خبر ہونے تک

پر تو خور سے' ہے شبنم کو فنا کی تعلیم   میں بھی ہوں' ایک عنایت کی نظر ہونے تک

یک نظر بیش نہیں' فرصتِ ہستی غافل   گرمیِ بزم' ہے اک رقصِ شرر ہونے تک

غمِ ہستی کا' اسد! کس سے ہو جز مرگ علاج

شمع ہر رنگ میں جلتی ہے سحر ہونے تک

25

When the day Comes

One can sigh, but a lifetime is needed to finish it.
We'll die before we see the tangles in your hair loosened.

There are dangers in waves, in all those crocodiles with their
    jaws open.
The drop of water goes through many difficulties before
    it becomes a pearl.

Love requires waiting, but desire doesn't want to wait.
The heart has no patience; but it would rather bleed to death.

I know you will respond when you understand the state of
    my soul,
But I'll probably become earth before all that is clear to you.

When the sun arrives the dew on the petal passes through
    the existence.
I am also me until your kind eye catches sight of me.

How long is your life? How long does an eyelash flutter?
The warmth of a poetry gathering is like a single spark.

Oh Ghalib, the sorrows of existence, what can cure them but
    death?
There are so many colors in the candle flame, and then
    the day comes.

मेरा सर, मेरे घुटनों पर

घर हमारा जो न रोते भी तो वीरां होता
बहर गर बहर न होता तो बयाबां होता

तंगी-ए-दिल का ग़िला क्या, ये तो क़ाफ़िर दिल है
कि अगर तंग न होता तो परीशां होता

बादे-यक-उमर-वरअ् बार तो देता बारे
काश, रिज़वां ही दरे-यार का दरबां होता

न था कुछ तो ख़ुदा था, कुछ होता तो ख़ुदा होता
डुबोया मुझको होने ने, न होता मैं तो क्या होता

हुआ जब ग़म से यूं बेहिस, तो ग़म क्या सर के कटने का
न होता गर जुदा तन से तो ज़ानू पर धरा होता

हुई मुद्दत कि 'ग़ालिब' मर गया पर याद आता है
वो हर इक बात पर कहना, कि यों होता तो क्या होता?

نہ ہوتا گر جدا تن سے تو زانو پر دھرا ہوتا

گھر ہمارا، جو نہ روتے بھی، تو ویراں ہوتا
بحر گر بحر نہ ہوتا، تو بیاباں ہوتا

تنگئ دل کا گلہ کیا؟ یہ وہ کافر دل ہے
کہ اگر تنگ نہ ہوتا، تو پریشاں ہوتا

بعد یک عمر ورع، بار تو دیتا، بارے
کاش! رضواں ہی درِ یار کا درباں ہوتا

نہ تھا کچھ، تو خدا تھا، کچھ نہ ہوتا تو خدا ہوتا
ڈبویا مجھ کو ہونے نے، نہ ہوتا میں، تو کیا ہوتا!

ہوا جب غم سے یوں بے حس تو غم کیا سر کے کٹنے کا؟
نہ ہوتا گر جدا تن سے، تو زانو پر دھرا ہوتا

ہوئی مدّت کہ، غالب! مر گیا، پر یاد آتا ہے

وہ ہر اک بات پر کہنا کہ، یوں ہوتا، تو کیا ہوتا؟

29

My Head and My Knees

If I didn't cry all the time, my house would still be desolate.
The ocean is huge and empty, just like the desert.

Am I to compalin about the narrowness of my heart?
It's unbelieving; no matter what happened, it would have
    been confused.

If I were patient for a lifetime, the Doorkeeper would surely
    let me in.
The doorkeeper of your house could model itself on such
    a heart.

Before anything, there was God; had there been nothing,
    there would have been God.
It was because I lived that I died. If I had never lived,
    what would have become of me?

Sorrow stunned my head; so why should I feel bad about my
    beheading?
If it hadn't been detached , it would be resting on my
    knees anyway.

Ghalib died centuries ago. But we still remember his little
    questions:
"What is before?" "Where would I be if I had never been
    born?"

हदों का मतलब

है बस कि हर इक उनके इशारे में निशां और
करते हैं मोहब्बत तो गुजरता है गुमां और

या रब वो न समझे हैं, न समझेंगे मेरी बात,
दे और दिल उनको, जो न दे मुझको ज़बाँ और

अबरु से है क्या उस निगहे-नाज़ को पैवंद
है तीर मुक़र्रर, मगर उसकी है कमां और

तुम शहर में हो तो हमें क्या ग़म? जब उठेंगे
ले आयेंगे बाज़ार से जाकर दिलो-जां और

हरचन्द सुबुक-दस्त हुए बुत-शिकनी में
हम हैं तो अभी राह में हैं संगे-गिरां और

है खूने-जिगर जोश में, दिल खोल के रोता
होते कई जो दीदा-ए-खूंनाबा-फ़िशां और

मरता हूँ इस आवाज़ पे, हरचन्द सर उड़ जाए
जल्लाद को लेकिन वो कहे जाएं कि 'हां और'

लोगों को है खुर्शिदे-जहां-ताब का धोका,
हर रोज दिखाता हूँ मैं इक दाग़े-निहां और

लेता, न अगर दिल तुम्हें देता, कोई दम चैन
करता, जो न मरता, कोई दिन आहो-फुग़ां और

पाते नहीं जब राह, तो चढ़ जाते हैं नाले
रुकती है मेरी तब्अ, तो होती है रवां और

हैं और भी दुनिया में सुख़नवर बहुत अच्छे,
कहते हैं कि 'ग़ालिब' का है अनदाज़े बयां और

دے اور دل ان کو جو نہ دے مجھ کو زباں اور

ہے بس کہ' ان کے اشارے میں نشاں اور
کرتے ہیں محبت' تو گزرتا ہے گماں اور

یارب! وہ نہ سمجھے ہیں' نہ سمجھیں گے مری بات
دے اور دل ان کو' جو نہ دے مجھ کو زباں اور

ابرو سے ہے کیا' اس نگہ کو ناز کو' پیوند؟
ہے تیر مقرر' مگر اس کو ہے کماں اور

تم شہر میں ہو' تو ہمیں کیا غم؟ جب اٹھیں گے
لے آئیں گے بازار سے' جاکر دل و جاں اور

ہر چند سبک دست ہوئے' بت شکنی میں'
ہم ہیں' تو ابھی راہ میں ہے سنگِ گراں اور

ہے خون جگر جوش میں' دل کھول کے روتا
ہوتے جو کئی دیدۂ خوں نا بہ فشاں اور

مرتا ہوں اس آواز پہ' ہر چند سر اڑ جائے
جلاد کو' لیکن' وہ کہے جائیں کہ "ہاں' اور"

لوگوں کو ہے خورشید جہاں تاب کا دھوکا
ہر روز دکھاتا ہوں میں اِک داغِ نہاں اور

لیتا' نہ اگر دل تمہیں دیتا' کوئی دم چین
کرتا' جو نہ مرتا' کوئی دن آہ و فغاں اور

پاتے نہیں جب راہ' تو چڑھ جاتے ہیں نالے
رُکتی ہے مری طبع' تو ہوتی ہے رواں اور

ہیں اور بھی دنیا میں سخنور بہت اچھے
کہتے ہیں کہ' غالب کا ہے انداز بیاں اور

About Limits and Meanings

When the Great One gestures to me, the message does not
    become clear.
When love words are spoken , I get six or seven meanings.

I must tell you, God, this woman doesn't grasp my meaning.
Give her a second heart, please, if you don't give me a
    second tongue.

Her eyebrows do make a bow, but the rest is unclear.
What are her eyes? An arrow or something else?

You come into town, and I still grieve. Of course I can go
To the market and buy another heart and another life.

I'm good at smashing rocks with my head, but it looks as if
Someone on this street has been strewing boulders.

My soul is full and it would be good to drain the blood.
The problem is limits; I have only two eyes.

Even though my head flies off, I love to hear her voice
As she remarks to the executioner: "You're doing well."

People get a real sense of what the sun is like
When I let the light reflect off one of my scars.

I could have had some peace, had I not fallen in love with you.
If I hadn't died, I could have done a lot more crying and
    sighing.

A river keeps rising when its bed is not available.
When my nature becomes dammed, it just keeps moving.

We know there is more than one good poet in the world,
But the experts say that Ghalib's little jests are great.

न कर आज ख़िस्सत शराब में

कल के लिये कर आज न ख़िस्सत शराब में
यह सूए-ज़न है साक़ी-ए-कौसर के बाब में

रौ में है रख़्शे-उम्र, कहाँ देखिये थमे
न हाथ बाग पर है, न पा है रकाब में

इतना ही मुझको अपनी हक़ीक़त से बोअद है
जितना कि वहमे-ग़ैर से हूँ पेचोताब में

अस्ले-शुहूदो-शाहिदो-मशहूद एक है
हैराँ हूँ, फिर मुशाहिदा है किस हिसाब में

है मुश्तमिल नमूदे-सुबर पर वजूदे-बहर,
याँ क्या धरा है क़तरा-ओ-मौजो-हबाब में

आराइशे-जमाल से फ़ारिग़ नहीं हनोज़
पेशे-नज़र है आईना दाइम नक़ाब में

है ग़ैबे-ग़ैब, जिसको समझते हैं हम शुहूद,
हैं ख़्वाब में हनोज़, जो जागे हैं ख़्वाब में

'ग़ालिब' नदीमे-दोस्त से आती है बू-ए-दोस्त
मशग़ूले-हक़ हूं बन्दगी-ए-बूतुराब में

کل کے لئے کر آج نہ خست شراب میں

یہ سوئے ظن ہے ساقیِ کوثر کے باب میں	کل کے لئے کر آج نہ خست شراب میں
نے ہاتھ باگ پر ہے، نہ پاہے رکاب میں	رو میں ہے رخشِ عمر، کہاں، دیکھئے تھمے
جتنا کہ وہم غیر سے ہوں پیچ و تاب میں	اُتنا ہی مجھ کو اپنی حقیقت سے بعد ہے
حیراں ہوں، پھر مشاہدہ ہے کس حساب میں	اصل شہود و شاہد و مشہود ایک ہے
یاں کیا دھرا ہے قطرہ موج و حباب میں	ہے مشتمل نمودِ صُور پر وجود بحر
پیش نظر ہے آئینہ دائم نقاب میں	آرائشِ جمال سے فارغ نہیں ہنوز
ہیں خواب میں ہنوز، جو جاگے ہیں خواب میں	ہے غیبِ غیب، جس کو سمجھتے ہیں ہم شہود

غالبؔ! ندیم دوست سے آتی ہے بوٍے دوست

مشغولِ حق ہوں، بندگیِ بوتراب میں

Don't Skimp with me Today

For tomorrow's sake, don't skimp with me on wine today.
A stingy portion implies a suspicion of heaven's abundance.

The horse of life is galloping; we'll never know the stopping place.
Our hands are not touching the reins, nor our feet the stirrups.

I keep a certain distance from the reality of things.
It's the same distance betweeen me and utter confusion.

The scene, the one looking, and the ability to see are all the same.
If that is so, why am I confused about what is in front of me?

The greatness of a river depends on its magnificent face.
If we break it into bubbles and drops and waves, we are lost.

She is not free from her ways to increase her beauty.
The mirror she sees is on the inside of her veil.

What we think is obvious is so far beyond our comprehension.
We are still dreaming even when we dream we are awake.

From the smell of my friend's friend I get the smell of my friend.
Listen, Ghalib, you are busy worshiping God's friend.

ख्वाहिशों का सफ़र

हैरा हूँ दिल को रोऊं कि पीटूं जिगर को मैं
मक़दूर हो तो साथ रखूं नौहागर को मैं

छोडा न रश्क ने, कि तेरे घर का नाम लूं
हर इक से पूछता हूं कि जाऊं किधर को मैं

जाना पडा, रक़ीब के दर पर हज़ार बार
ऐ काश, जानता न तेरी रहगुज़र को मैं

लो वह भी कहते हैं कि यह बे-नंगो नाम है
यह जानता अगर, तो लुटाता न घर को मैं

ख़्वाहिश को अहमकों ने परसतिश दिया क़रार
क्या पूजता हूं उस बुते-बेदादगर को मैं

चलता हूं थोडी दूर, हर इक तेज रौ के साथ,
पहचानता नहीं हूं अभी राहबर को मैं

फिर बेखुदी मे भूल गया, राहे-कूए-यार
जाता वगरना एक दिन अपनी ख़बर को मैं

अपने पे कर रहा हूं कयास अहले-दहर का
समझा हूं दिल-पज़ीर मता-ए-हुनर को मैं

حیراں ہوں دل کو روؤں کہ پیٹوں جگر کو میں

حیراں ہوں دل کو روؤں کہ پیٹوں جگر کو میں

مقدور ہو، تو ساتھ رکھوں نوحہ گر کو میں

چھوڑا نہ رشک نے کہ، ترے گھر کا نام لوں

ہر اک سے پوچھتا ہوں کہ "جاؤں کدھر کو میں؟"

جانا پڑا رقیب کے در پر، ہزار بار

اے کاش! جانتا نہ تری رہگزر کو میں!

لو، وہ بھی کہتے ہیں کہ "کہ بے ننگ و نام ہے"

یہ جانتا اگر، تو لٹاتا نہ گھر کو میں

چلتا ہوں تھوڑی دُور، ہر اک تیز رو کے ساتھ

پہچانتا نہیں ہوں ابھی راہبر کو میں

خواہش کو، احمقوں نے پرستش دیا قرار

کیا پوجتا ہوں اس بُت بیداد گر کو میں

پھر بیخودی میں بھول گیا، راہِ کوے یار

جاتا و گرنا ایک دن اپنی خبر کو میں

اپنے پہ کر رہا ہوں قیاس، اہلِ دہر کا

سمجھا ہوں دل پذیر، متاعِ ہنر کو میں

41

Fantasies and Jealousies

I am confused: should I cry over my heart, or slap my
    chest?
If I could afford it, I'd have a man paid to cry.

My jealousy is so strong that I refuse to name the street where
    you live.
In view of that, "How do I get there?" doesn't make
    much sense.

I was forced to walk to his house a thousand times.
I wish I'd never known about that path you like so
    much.

It's clear to her that my fate is nothing and nobody.
If I had known that, I would not have thrown away my
    house.

Fools typically mistake simple desire for a form of worship.
Do I desire a hard woman or do I worship a stone?

I walk for a short distance with each fast-moving stream.
But that's because I don't know who the guide is.

I was so carefree I forgot the roads to my friend's house.
Now how can I discover who am I?

I judge the whole world on the basis of my imagination.
I think that every person loves a true work of art.

कुछ सवाल

जबकि तुझ बिन नहीं कोई मौजूद,
फिर ये हंगामा, ऐ ख़ुदा! क्या है?

ये परी-चेहरा लोग कैसे हैं
गम्ज़ा-ओ-इश्वा-ओ-अदा क्या है

सब्ज़ा-ओ-गुल कहां से आये हैं?
अबर क्या चीज़ है, हवा क्या है

हमको उनसे वफा की है उम्मीद
जो नहीं जानते वफा क्या है

हां, भला कर, तेरा भला होगा
और दरवेश की सदा क्या है

जान तुझ पर निसार करता हूँ
मैं नहीं जानता दुआ क्या है

मैंने माना कि कुछ नहीं 'ग़ालिब'
मुफ्त हाथ आये तो बुरा क्या है

پھر یہ ہنگامہ اے خدا کیا ہے

جب کہ تجھ بن نہیں کوئی موجود   پھر یہ ہنگامہ اے خدا' کیا ہے؟

یہ پری چہرہ لوگ کیسے ہیں؟   غمزہ و عشوہ و ادا کیا ہے؟

سبزہ و گل کہاں سے آئے ہیں؟   ابر کیا چیز ہے؟ ہوا کیا ہے؟

ہم کو ان سے' وفا کی ہے امید   جو نہیں جانتے' وفا کیا ہے؟

ہاں بھلا کر' ترا بھلا ہوگا   اور درویش کی صدا کی ہے؟

جان تم پر نثار کرتا ہوں   میں نہیں جانتا' دعا کیا ہے؟

میں نے مانا کہ کچھ نہیں غالب

مفت ہاتھ آئے تو برا کیا ہے؟

Questions

Since nothing actually exists except You,
Then why do I keep hearing all this noise?

These magnificent women with their beauty astound me.
Their side-glances, their eyebrows, how does all that
    work? What is it?

These palm trees and these tulips, where did they come from?
What purpose do they serve? What are clouds and wind?

We hope for faithfulness and loyalty from people.
But people don't have the faintest idea what loyalty is.

Good rises from good actions, and that is good.
Beyond that, what else do saints and good people say?

I am willing to give up my breath and my life for you,
Even though I don't know the first thing about sacrifice.

The abundant objects of the world mean nothing at all!
But if the wine is free, how could Ghalib hold back?

होता है शबो रोज़ तमाशा मेरे आगे

बाज़ीचा-ए-अतफ़ाल है दुनिया मेरे आगे
होता है शबो-रोज़ तमाशा मेरे आगे

इक खेल है औरंगे-सुलेमां मेरे नज़दीक
इक बात है ऐजाज़े-मसीहा मेरे आगे

जुज़ नाम नहीं सूरते-आलम मुझे मंज़ूर
जुज़ वहम नहीं हस्ती-ए-अशिया मेरे आगे

होता है निहां गर्द में सहरा मेरे होते
घिसता है जबीं ख़ाक पे दरिया मेरे आगे

मत पूछ कि क्या हाल है मेरा तेरे पीछे
तू देख कि क्या रंग है तेरा मेरे आगे

सच कहते हो, ख़ुदबीनो-ख़ुदआरा न क्यों हूँ
बैठा है बुते-आईना-सीमा मेरे आगे

फिर देखिये अनदाज़े-गुल अफ़शानी-ए-गुफ़्तार
रख दे कोई पैमाना-ओ-सहबा मेरे आगे

नफ़रत का गुमां गुज़रे है, मैं रश्क से गुज़रा
क्योंकर कहूँ, लो नाम न उनका मेरे आगे

ईमां मुझे रोके है, तो खींचें है मुझे कुफ्र
काबा मेरे पीछे है, कलीसा मेरे आगे

49

आशिक हूँ, पे माशूक-फरेबी है मेरा काम
मजनूं को बुरा कहती है लैला मेरे आगे

खुश होते हैं पर वस्ल में यों मर नहीं जाते
आई शबे-हिजरां की तमन्ना मेरे आगे

है मौजज़न इक कुल्जुमे खूं, काश यही हो
आता है अभी देखिये क्या-क्या मेरे आगे

गो हाथ को जुंबिश नहीं, आंखों में तो दम है
रहने दो अभी साग़ारों-मीना मेरे आगे

हम-पेशा-ओ-हम-मशरबो हम-राज़ है मेरा
'ग़ालिब' को बुरा क्यों कहो, अच्छा मेरे आगे

ہوتا ہے شب و روز تماشا مرے آگے

بازیچۂ اطفال ہے دنیا، مرے آگے

ہوتا ہے شب و روز تماشا مرے آگے

ایک کھیل ہے اورنگِ سلیماں مرے نزدیک

اے بات ہے اعجازِ مسیحا، مرے آگے

جز نام، نہیں صورتِ عالم مجھے منظور

جز وہم، نہیں ہستی اشیا مرے آگے

ہوتا ہے نہاں گرد میں صحرا، مرے ہوتے

گھستا ہے جبیں خاک پہ دریا، مرے آگے

مت پوچھ کہ، کیا حال ہے میرا ترے پیچھے

تو دیکھ کہ، کیا رنگ ہے تیرا، مرے آگے

سچ کہتے ہو، خودبین و خود آرا ہوں کیوں نہ ہوں؟

بیٹھا ہے بت آئنہ سیما، مرے آگے

پھر دیکھیے، اندازِ گل افشانیِ گفتار

رکھ دے کوئی، پیمانۂ صہبا مرے آگے

نفرت کا گماں گزرے ہے، میں رشک سے گزرا

کیوں کر کہوں "لو نام نہ ان کا مرے آگے"

ایماں مجھے روکے ہے، جو کھینچے ہے مجھے کفر

کعبہ مرے پیچھے ہے، کلیسا مرے آگے

عاشق ہوں، پہ معشوق فریبی ہے مرا کام

مجنوں کو بُرا کہتی ہے لیلا، مرے آگے

خوش ہوتے ہیں، پر وصل میں یوں مر نہیں جاتے

آئی شبِ ہجراں کی تمنا، مرے آگے

ہے موجزن اک قلزمِ خوں، کاش! یہی ہو

آتا ہے، ابھی دیکھیے، کیا کیا مرے آگے

گو ہاتھ کو جنبش نہیں آنکھوں میں تو دم ہے

رہنے دو ابھی ساغر و مینا مرے آگے

ہم پیشہ و ہم مشرب و ہم راز ہے میرا

غالبؔ کو بُرا کیوں کہو، اچھا مرے آگے

Some Exaggerations

The world I see looks to me like a game of children.
Strange performances and plays go on night and day.

King Solomon's throne is not a big thing to me.
The miracles of Jesus are basically a topic of conversation.

The idea that the world exists is not acceptable to me.
Illusion is real, but not the things of the world.

The desert covers its head with sand when I appear with my
    troubles.
The river rubs its forehead in the mud when it sees me.

Don't ask me how I am when I am parted from you.
I notice that your face turns a little pale when you're
    near me.

People are right to say that I love looking at myself, but sitting
In front of me is a beauty whose face is bright as a
    mirror.

Just put a wineglass and some wine in front of me;
Words will fall out of my mouth like apple blossoms.

People imagine that I hate, but it's merely jealousy.
That's why I scream: "Don't say her name in my presence!"

Faith pulls me in one direction, but disbelief pulls me in
    another.
The Kaaba stands far behind me, and the Church stands
    next to me.

I am a lover; therefore charming a woman is my work.
When she is near me, Laila makes fun of Majnoon.

The time of reunion brings happiness rather than death.
When reunion came, I remembered the night of parting.

We have a sea of blood now with large waves.
I am content with it; I know worse could happen.

My hands move with difficulty, but atleast my eyes are lively.
Just leave the glass and the wine jug standing where
    they are.

Ghalib is a Muslim also, so we know a lot of each other's
    secrets.
Please don't speak badly of Ghalib when I'm around.

Part II

इंतज़ारे-खुदा

मिलती है खूए-यार से नार इल्तिहाब में
क़ाफ़िर हूँ गर न मिलती हो राहत अज़ाब में

कब से हूं क्या बताऊं जहाने-ख़राब में
शब-हाए-हिज़्र को भी रखूं गर हिसाब में

ता फिर न इंतज़ार में नींद आए उमर भर
आने का अहद कर गए, आये जो ख़्वाब में

क़ासिद के आते-आते, ख़त इक और लिख रखूँ
मैं जानता हूँ जो वो लिखेंगे जवाब में

मुझ तक कब उनकी बज़्म में आता था दौरे-ज़ाम
साक़ी ने कुछ मिला न दिया हो शराब में

जो मुन्किरे-वफ़ा हो, फ़रेब उस पे क्या चले
क्यों बदगुमां हूँ दोस्त से, दुश्मन के बाब में

मैं मुज़्तरिब हूँ वस्ल में ख़ौफ़े-रक़ीब से
डाला है तुमको वहम ने किस पेचो-ताब में

लाखों लगाव, इक चुराना निगाह का
लाखों बनाव, इक बिगड़ना इताब में

वो सेहर मुद्दआ-तलबी में न काम आए
जिस सेहर से सफ़ीना रवां हो सराब में

'ग़ालिब' छुटी शराब, पर अब भी कभी-कभी
पीता हूँ रोज़े-अब्रो-शबे-माहताब में

کافر ہوں گر نہ ملتی ہو راحت عذاب میں

کافر ہوں، گر نہ ملتی ہو راحت عذاب میں

ملتی ہے خوے یار سے نار' التہاب میں

شبہائے ہجر کو بھی رکھوں گر حساب میں

کب سے ہوں' کیا بتاؤں' جہانِ خراب میں

آنے کا عہد کر گئے' آئے جو خواب میں

تا پھر نہ انتظار میں نیند آئے عمر بھر

میں جانتا ہوں' جو وہ لکھیں گے جواب میں

قاصد کے آتے آتے' خط اک اور لکھ رکھوں

ساقی نے کچھ ملا نہ دیا ہو شراب میں

مجھ تک کہ کب' ان کی بزم میں آتا تھا دورِ جام!

کیوں بدگماں ہوں دوست سے دشمن کے باب میں

جو منکرِ وفا ہو' فریب اس پہ کیا چلے

ڈالا ہے تم کو وہم نے' کس پیچ و تاب میں

میں مضطرب ہوں وصل میں' خوفِ رقیب سے

لاکھوں بناؤ' ایک بگڑنا عتاب میں

لاکھوں لگاؤ' ایک چرانا نگاہ کا

جس سحر سے سفینہ رواں رواں ہو سراب میں

وہ سحر' مدعا طلبی میں نہ کام آئے!

غالب! چھٹی شراب! پر اب بھی کبھی کبھی

پیتا ہوں روزِ ابر و شبِ ماہ تاب میں

Waiting for God

My lover's temperament resembles the fires of the hell.
I must be an unbeliever, because I enjoy this burning.

It's hard to say how long I've been in this wasteland,
Especially if I count the nights of separation.

Let there be no more sleep ever, because she promised
In my dream she would meet me in real life.

My message hasn't received a reply so I guess I'll write
    another.
I think I know what the Great One will say anyway.

In her poetry gatherings, the Great One never passes the cup
    to me.
Now I hold it; I hope no one has mixed anything in the
    wine.

How can you cheat someone who doesn't even accept the
    concept of love?
If I have a rival, it's mad of me to be jealous of him.

At the moment of reunion with her, I think of my rival.
My suspicion has taken away the joy of her presence.

How many loves can match the moment she turns her glance
    away?
How many gold rings can match one instant of her anger?

When we watch a mirage, ships appear to sail forward.
Such magic will be no help to me in achieving what I want.

Ghalib, we've given up wine; but sometimes we still do drink,
For example, on cloudy days or nights of the full moon.

रात पी ज़मज़म पे मे

ग़ैर लें महफिल में बोसे जाम के
हम रहें यूं तिश्ना-लब पैग़ाम के

ख़स्तगी का तुमसे क्या शिकवा कि ये
हथकण्डे हैं चर्ख़-नीली-फाम के

ख़त लिखेंगे, गर्चे मतलब कुछ न हो
हम तो आशिक हैं तुम्हारे नाम के

रात पी ज़मज़म पे मै और सुब्ह दम
धोये धब्बे जामा-ए-अहराम के

दिल को आंखों ने फंसाया क्या मगर
ये भी हल्के हैं तुम्हारे दाम के

इश्क ने 'ग़ालिब' निक्कमा कर दिया
वर्ना हम भी आदमी थे काम के

رات پی زمزم پہ مے اور صبح دم

ہم رہیں یوں تشنہ لب پیغام کے   غیر لیں محفل میں، بوسے جام کے

ہتھکنڈے ہیں چرخِ نیلی فام میں   ختگی کا تم سے کیا شکوہ کہ یہ

ہم تو عاشق ہیں، تمہارے نام کے   خط لکھیں گے، گرچہ مطلب کچھ نہ ہو

دھوئے دھبّے جامہ احرام کے   رات پی زمزم پہ مے اور صبح دم

یہ بھی حلقے ہیں تمہارے دام کے   دل کو آنکھوں نے پھنسایا، کیا مگر

عشق نے غالبؔ! نکما کردیا

ورنہ ہم بھی آدمی تھے کام کے

63

Near the Zam Zam Well

Others in your poetry gathering kiss the wine cup;
But we remain thirsty even for the invitation.

I won't complain about the way I'm being destroyed.
It must be a trick that the blue sky is playing on me.

I'll write this letter even though it may not have a message.
I'll send it just because I'm a lover of your name.

I drank wine that night near the well of Zam Zam,
And in the morning washed wine stains from my pilgrim's
    robe.

My own eyes have formed the loops in your net.
It's possible my heart had no choice but to be caught.

Ghalib, love has made you absolutely useless.
At one time Ghalib was useful for something.

राहे पुर ख़ार

क्यों जल गया न ताबे-रुख़े-यार देखकर?
जलता हूं अपनी ताक़ते-दीदार देखकर

आतिश परस्त कहते हैं, अहले-जहां मुझे
सरगर्मे-नाला-हाए-शरर-बार देखकर

आता है मेरे कत्ल को, पर जोशे-रश्क से
मरता हूँ उसके हाथ में तलवार देखकर

वा हसरता कि यार ने खैंचा सितम से हाथ
हमको हरीसे-लज़्ज़ते-आज़ार देखकर

साबित हुआ है, गर्देने-मीना पे ख़ूने-ख़ल्क
लरजै है मौजे-मै तेरी रफ्तार देखकर

बिक जाते हैं हम आप, मता-ए-सुख़न के साथ
लेकिन, अयारे-तब:-ए-ख़रीदार देखकर

इन आबलों से पाँव के घबरा गया था मैं
जी ख़ुश हुआ है राह को पुर-ख़ार देखकर

गिरनी थी हम पर बर्क़े-तजल्ली, न तूर पर
देतें हैं बादा, ज़र्फ़े-क़दह:-ख़्वार देखकर

جی خوش ہوا راہ کو پر خار دیکھ کر

کیوں جل گیا نہ تابِ رُخِ یار دیکھ کر؟   جلتا ہوں، اپنی طاقتِ دیدار دیکھ کر

آتش پرست کہتے ہیں اہلِ جہاں مجھے   سرگرم نالہائے شرر بار دیکھ کر

آتا ہے میرے قتل کو، پر جوش رشک سے   مرتا ہوں، اس کے ہاتھ میں تلوار دیکھ کر

ثابت ہوا ہے، گردنِ مینا پہ، خونِ خلق   لرزے ہے موجِ مے، تری رفتار دیکھ کر

واحسرتا! کہ یار نے کھینچا ستم سے ہاتھ   ہم کو حریص لذتِ آزار دیکھ کر

بک جاتے ہیں ہم آپ، متاعِ سخن کے ساتھ   لیکن، عیارِ طبع خریدار دیکھ کر

ان آبلوں سے پانو کے، گھبرا گیا تھا میں   جی خوش ہوا ہے، راہ کو پُر خار دیکھ کر

گرنی تھی ہم پہ برقِ تجلی، نہ طور پر

دیتے ہیں بادہ، ظرفِ قدح خوار دیکھ کر

The Road with Thorns

Why didn't I burn when I saw the heat on the face of the
    Great One?
My eyes did see Her; now I'm envious of my own eyes.

The world believes that I am a fire-worshiper
Because when I cry flames leap out of my eyes.

The Great One comes to kill me-but I am so jealous
I die just glancing at the sword She is holding.

It's sad that She pulled her hand away from my torture.
She did that because She could see that I was enjoying
    that.

Wine kills the world; blame the mouth of the pitcher for that.
Even wine quivers when it sees your beauty go by.

There's a way we sell even our deepest poetry,
But only after we've checked the depth of the benefactor.

I was afraid to walk because I had blisters on my feet.
Now I see the road is filled with thorns; that makes me
    happy.

The lightning that fell on Moses should have fallen on Ghalib.
You know we always adjust the amount of the wine to
    the quality of the drinker.

क़तरा जो दरिया न हुआ

दरख़ुरे-क़हरो-ग़ज़ब जब कोई हम सा न हुआ
फिर ग़लत क्या है कि हम सा कोई पैदा न हुआ

बन्दगी में भी वह आज़ाद-ओ-खुदबीं हैं कि हम
उल्टे फिर आयें दरे-काबा अगर वा न हुआ

सबको मक़बूल है दावा तेरी यकताई का
रुबरु कोई बुते-आईना-सीमा न हुआ

सीने का दाग़ है वो नाला कि लब तक न गया
ख़ाक का रिज़्क़ है वो क़तरा जो दरिया न हुआ

क़तरा में दजला दिखाई न दे और जुज़्व में कुल
खेल लड़कों का हुआ दीदा-ए-बीना न हुआ

हर बुने-मू से दमे-ज़िक्र न टपके खूंनाब
हम्ज़ा का किस्सा हुआ, इश्क़ का चर्चा न हुआ

थी ख़बर गर्म कि ग़ालिब के उड़ेंगे पुरज़े
देखने हम भी गए थे, पे तमाशा न हुआ

خاک کا رزق ہے وہ قطرہ کہ دریا نہ ہوا

در خورِ قہر و غضب، جب کوئی ہم سا نہ ہوا   پھر غلط کیا ہے کہ، ہم سا کوئی پیدا نہ ہوا

بندگی میں بھی، وہ آزاد و خود بیں ہیں کہ ہم   الٹے پھر آئے، درِ کعبہ اگر وا نہ ہوا

سب کو مقبول ہے دعویٰ تری یکتائی کا   روبرو کوئی بُتِ آئنہ سیما نہ ہوا

سینہ کا داغ، ہے وہ نالہ کہ، لب تک نہ گیا   خاک کا رزق، ہے وہ قطرہ کہ دریا نہ ہوا

قطرہ میں دجلہ دکھائی نہ دے، اور جزو میں کل   کھیل لڑکوں کا ہوا، دیدۂ بینا نہ ہوا

ہر بُن مُو سے دم ذکر نہ ٹپکے خوناب   حمزہ کا قصہ ہوا، عشق کا چرچا نہ ہوا

تھی خبر گرم کہ غالب کے اُڑیں گے پرزے

دیکھنے ہم بھی گئے تھے، پہ تماشا نہ ہوا

The Drop and the River

No one anywhere can equal me in accepting your torture.
It's not an overstatement to say there's no one like me.

Even when religious we are so egotistical we'll turn around
And go home if the door to the Kaaba is not open.

Everyone accepts your claim that you are the Only One.
That being so, an image of you is utterly impossible.

If you don't complain out loud there'll be a stain on the heart.
The drop that doesn't become the river will be eaten by
    the sand.

If you can't see the Ganges in a drop and the planet in a grain
    of sand,
Then your eyes are not adult but the eyes of infants.

While telling the story, if each eyelash doesnot drip with
    blood
You're not telling a love story, but a tale made for the
    kids.

Gossip was that when Ghalib spoke, he would be broken with
    insults.
He too went to watch that event, but it turned out differently.

मुश्किल है कलाम मेरा

मुश्किल है ज़बस कलाम मेरा ऐ दिल।
सुन-सुन के उसे सुख़नवराने-कामिल

आसान कहने की करते हैं फ़रमाइश
गोयम मुश्किल वगर्ना गोयम मुश्किल

مشکل ہے زبس کلام میرا اے دل

مشکل ہے زبس کلام میرا اے دل!   سُن سُن کے اسے سخنورانِ کامل

آسان کہنے کی کرتے ہیں فرمایش   گویم مشکل و گر نہ گویم مشکل

About My Poems

I agree, O heart, that my ghazals are not easy to take in.
When they hear my work, experienced poets

Tell me I should write something easier to understand.
I have to write what's difficult, otherwise it is difficult to
  write.

जबीं पे सजदा ए बुत का निशां नहीं

हम पर ज़फा से तर्के-वफ़ा का गुमां नहीं
इक छेड़ है वगर्ना मुराद इम्तिहां नहीं

किस मुंह से शुक्र कीजिये इस लुत्फ़े-खास का
पुरसिश है और पाए-सुख़न दरमियां नहीं

हमको सितम अज़ीज़, सितमगर को हम अज़ीज़
ना-मेहरबां नहीं है, अगर मेहरबां नहीं

बोसा नहीं, न दीजिये, दुश्नाम ही सही
आखिर ज़बां तो रखते हो तुम, गर दहां नहीं

ख़ंजर से चीर सीना, अगर दिल न हो दोनीम
दिल में छुरी चुभो, मिज़ां गर ख़ूँचकां नहीं

है नंगे-सीना, दिल अगर आतिश-कदा न हो
है आरे-दिल नफ़स अगर आज़र-फ़िशां नहीं

नुकसां नहीं जुनूं में, बला से हो घर खराब
सौ गज़ ज़मीं के बदले, बयाबाँ गराँ नहीं

कहते हो क्या लिखा है तेरी सरनविश्त में
गोया जबीं पे सजदा-ए-बुत का निशां नहीं

पाता हूँ उससे दाद कुछ अपने कलाम की
रुह-उल-कुदुस अगर्चे मेरा हमज़बां नहीं

जां है बहाए-बोसा वले क्यों कहे अभी
'ग़ालिब' को जानता है कि वो नीमजां नहीं

گویا جبیں یہ سجدۂ بت کا نشان نہیں

اک چھیڑ ہے' وگرنہ مُراد امتحاں نہیں	ہم پر' جفا سے' ترکِ وفا کا گماں نہیں
پُرسش ہے اور پاے سخن درمیاں نہیں	کس منہ سے شکر کیجے' اس لطف خاص کا!
نا مہرباں نہیں ہے' اگر مہربان نہیں	ہم کو ستمگر عزیز' ستمگر کو ہم عزیز
آخر زباں تو رکھتے ہو تم گر دہاں نہیں	بوسہ نہیں' نہ دیجے' دُشنام ہی سہی
دل میں چھری چھبو' مژہ گر خونچکاں نہیں	خنجر سے چیر سینہ' اگر دل نہ ہو دو نیم
ہے عارِ دل' نفس اگر آزر فشاں نہیں	ہے تنگِ سینہ' دل اگر آتش کدہ نہ ہو
سو گز زمیں کے بدلے' بیاباں گراں نہیں	نقصاں نہیں جنوں میں' بلا سے ہو گھر خراب
گویا جبیں یہ سجدۂ بُت کا نشاں نہیں	کہتے ہو کیا لکھا ہے تری سرنوشت میں؟"
رُوح القُدُس اگرچہ' مرا ہم زباں نہیں	پاتا ہوں اس سے داد کچھ اپنے کلام کی

جاں ہے بہاے بوسہ' ولے کیوں کہے' ابھی

غالبؔ کو جانتا ہے کہ وہ نیم جاں نہیں

Rubbing My Forehead

She has a habit of torture, but doesn't mean to end the love.
Such oppression is only teasing; we don't imagine it as a test.

Which of my mouths shall I use to thank her for this delight?
I know she inquires about me even though no word is
   exchanged.

The one who tortures likes us, and we like the torturers.
So if she's not kind, we have to say she's not unkind.

If you don't give me a kiss, at least curse at me.
That means you have a tongue if you don't have a mouth.

If your heart is still in one piece, cut your chest with a dagger.
If eyelashes are not soaked with blood, put a knife in
   your heart.

The heart is an embarrassment to the chest if it's not on fire.
Releasing a breath brings shame if it's not a fountain of
   flame.

Well, it's not a loss for me if my madness has destroyed our
   house.
Giving up a large house for a wilderness is a good bargain.

You ask me what is written on my forehead? It shows marks
From being rubbed on the stone floor before some god.

Gabriel sends praise to me for my poems;
That happens even though Gabriel speaks a different
   language.

For the price of one kiss she sets my whole life-
Because she knows Ghalib is only about half alive.

शमअ के हवाख़्वाह अहले बज़्म

दोनो जहान देके वो समझे ये खुश रहा
यां आ पड़ी ये शर्म कि तकरार क्या करें

थक-थक के हर मुकाम पे दो-चार रह गये
तेरा पता न पायें, तो नाचार क्या करें

क्या शमूअ के नहीं है हवाख़्वाह अहलेबज़्म
हो ग़म ही जांगुदाज़, तो ग़मख़्वार क्या करें

کیا شمع کے نہیں ہیں ہوا خواہ اہلِ بزم؟

دونوں جہان دے کے' وہ سمجھے' یہ خوش رہا   یاں آپڑی یہ شرم کہ' تکرار کیا کریں

تھک تھک کے' ہر مقام پہ دو چار رہ گئے   تیرا پتا نہ پائیں' تو ناچار کیا کریں؟

کیا شمع کے نہیں ہیں ہوا خواہ اہلِ بزم؟

ہو غم ہی جاں گداز' تو غم خوار کیا کریں؟

The Candle Flame

He gave me heaven and earth, and assumed I'd be satisfied,
Actually I was too embarrassed to argue.

The spiritual seekers are tired, two or three at each stage of
the path.
The rest-who have given up-never knew your address at all.

There are so many in this gathering who wish the candle well.
But if the being of the candle is melting, what can the
sorrow-sharers do?

तुफ़ान और चराग़

नाला जुज़ हुस्ने-तलब, ऐ सितम-ईजाद, नहीं
है तक़ाज़ा-ए-जफ़ा, शिकवा-ए-बेदाद नहीं

कम नहीं वो भी ख़राबी में, पै वुसअत मालूम
दश्त में है मुझे वो ऐश कि घर याद नहीं

अहले-बीनिश को है तुफ़ाने-हवादिस मकतब
लतमए-मौज कम-अज़-सेलिए-उस्ताद नहीं

वाए महरुमी-ए-तसलीमव बदा हाले-वफा
जानता है, कि हमें ताकते-फरियाद नहीं

रंगे-तमकीने-गुलो-लाला परीशाँ क्यों हैं
गर चराग़ाने-सरे-रह-गुज़रे-बाद नहीं

कम नहीं जल्वागरी में तेरे कूचे से बहिश्त
यही नक्शा है, वले, इस कदर आबाद नहीं

करते किस मुंह से हो गुर्बत की शिकायत 'ग़ालिब'
तुमको बे-मुहरी-ए-याराने-वतन याद नहीं

گر چراغانِ سرِ رہ گزر باد نہیں

ہے تقاضائے جفا، شکوۂ بیداد نہیں	نالہ جز حسنِ طلب، اے ستم ایجاد! نہیں
دشت میں، ہے مجھے وہ عیش کہ گھر یاد نہیں	کم نہیں وہ بھی خرابی میں، پہ وسعت معلوم
لطمہ موج، کم از سَیلی استاد، نہیں	اہلِ بینش کو، ہے طوفانِ حوادث، مکتب
جانتا ہے کہ، ہمیں طاقتِ فریاد نہیں	وائے محرومیِ تسلیم و بدا حالِ وفا!
گر چراغانِ سرِ رہ گزر باد نہیں	رنگِ تمکینِ گل و لالہ پریشان کیوں ہے؟
یہی نقشہ ہے، ولے اس قدر آباد نہیں	کم نہیں، جلوہ گری میں، ترے کوچے سے بہشت

کرتے کس منہ سے ہو، غربت کی شکایت غالب

تم کو بے مہریِ یارانِ وطن یاد نہیں؟

A Lamp in a Strong Wind

My wailing- oh inventor of torture-is just a mode of petition.
It's really a request for more torture, and not a complaint.

Even though my house is destroyed, I recognize the value of
    open space.
In the deliciousness of the desert I forget about home.

To the wise, a storm of difficulty may be a school.
The slaps of waves resemble the slaps of a master.

Things have gone so far that she doesn't even say hello.
If I complain to God, she knows my complaints have no
    effect.

Why are the roses and the tulips losing their elegant colors?
Maybe they recognize they are lamps in the path of a
    strong wind.

In the street where you live I see the splendor of Paradise.
But Paradise is not as crowded as your street.

Ghalib, which mouth are you using when you complain of
    your exile?
Have you forgotten the unkindness of people in your
    own city?

क़ासिद भी घबरा जाए है मुझसे

कभी नेकी भी उसके जी में गर आ जाये है मुझसे
जफ़ाएँ कर के अपनी याद शर्मा जाये है मुझसे

खुदाया। जज़्बा-ए-दिल की मगर तासीर उल्टी है
कि जितना खींचता हूं, और खिंचता जाए है मुझसे

वह बद-ख़ू, और मेरी दास्ताने-इश्क़ तूलानी
इबारत मुख़्तसर, क़ासिद भी घबरा जाए है मुझसे

उधर वह बदगुमानी है, इधर यह नातवानी है
न पूछा जाए है उससे, न बोला जाए है मुझसे

संभलने दे मुझें ए नाउम्मीदी क्या क़्यामत है
कि दामाने ख़्याले चार छूटा जाए है मुझसे

तकल्लुफ बरतरफ़, नज़्ज़ारगी में भी सही, लेकिन
वो देखा जाए, कब ये जुल्म देखा जाए है मुझसे

हुए हैं पाँव ही पहले नबुर्दे-ए-इश्क में ज़ख़्मी,
न भागा जाए है मुझसे, न ठहरा जाए है मुझसे

कयामत है, कि होवे मुद्दई का हमसफर, 'ग़ालिब'
वो काफ़िर, जो खुदा को भी न सौंपा जाए है मुझसे

قاصد بھی گھبرا جائے ہے مجھ سے

کبھی نیکی بھی اس کے جی میں گر آ جائے ہے، مجھ سے
جفائیں کرکے اپنی یاد، شرما جائے ہے مجھ سے

خدایا! جذبۂ دل کی مگر تاثیرات اُلٹی ہے
کہ جتنا کھینچتا ہوں اور کھنچتا جائے ہے، مجھ سے

وہ بدخو، اور میری داستانِ عشق طولانی
عبارت مختصر، قاصد بھی گھبرا جائے ہے، مجھ سے

اُدھر وہ بدگمانی ہے، اِدھر یہ ناتوانی ہے
نہ پوچھا جائے ہے اس سے، نہ بولا جائے ہے، مجھ سے

سنبھلنے دے مجھے، اے ناامیدی! کیا قیامت ہے
کہ دامانِ خیالِ یار، چھوٹا جائے ہے، مجھ سے

تکلف برطرف، نظارگی میں بھی سہی، لیکن
وہ دیکھا جائے، کب یہ ظلم دیکھا جائے ہے، مجھ سے

ہوئے ہیں پاؤں ہی پہلے، نبردِ عشق میں زخمی
نہ بھاگا جائے ہے مجھ سے، نہ ٹھہرا جائے ہے مجھ سے

قیامت ہے کہ، ہووے مدّعی کا ہم سفر، غالب
وہ کافر، جو خدا کو بھی نہ سونپا جائے ہے مجھ سے

When My Letter Writer Gets Frightened

Whenever a feeling of kindness toward me enters the ears of
  her heart
She recalls the old abuse she's given me and becomes shy.

God, I want to know why my desires bring the opposite effect.
The more I try to attract the Great One, the farther away
  she moves.

She is quick to anger, and my love messages take so long.
Even my letter writer looks apprehensive when I sit down.

On her side she is suspicious; on my side I am feeble.
So she never asks how I am, nor can I explain.

O despair, let me get settled now so I can see this catastrophe.
Even the shirt-tail of my vision of her is trying to escape.

The etiquette is that I can't tell people not to look at her.
I do look, but I can't tolerate that others should look at her.

In the first skirmish of the love battle, I got wounded in the feet.
Now I can neither run away nor remain standing up.

Ghalib, this is the Last day. We are sharing a path with my
  rival—
That infidel no one could trust even in God's presence.

हजारो ख़्वाहिशें

हजारों ख़्वाहिशें ऐसी, कि हर ख़्वाहिश पे दम निकले
बहुत निकले मेरे अरमान, लेकिन फिर भी कम निकले

डरे क्यों मेरा क़ातिल, क्या रहेगा उसकी गर्दन पर
वो खूं, जो चश्मे-तर-से उम्र-भर यूं दम-ब-दम निकले

निकलना खुल्द से आदम का सुनते आये थे लेकिन
बहुत बेआबरू होकर तेरे कूचे से हम निकले

भरम खुल जाए ज़ालिम तेरे क़ामत की दराज़ी का
अगर इस तुर्रा-ए-पुर-पेचोख़म का पेचोख़म निकल

मगर लिखवाए कोई उसको ख़त, तो हमसे लिखवाए
हुई सुब्ह और घर से कान पर रखकर कलम निकले

हुई इस दौर में मंसूब मुझसे बादा-आशामी
फिर आया वो ज़माना, जो जहां में जामे-जम निकले

हुई जिनसे तवक्क़ो ख़स्तगी की दाद पाने की
वो हमसे भी ज़ियादा ख़स्ता-ए-तेग़े सितम निकले

मोहब्बत में नहीं है फ़र्क़ जीने का और मरने का
उसी को देखकर जीते हैं जिस काफ़िर पे दम निकले

खुदा के वास्ते पर्दा न काबे का उठा ज़ालिम
कहीं ऐसा न हो यां भी वही काफ़िर सनम निकले

कहां मैखाने का दरवाज़ा 'गालिब', और कहां वाईज़
पर इतना जानते हैं, कल वो जाता था कि हम निकले

94

ہزاروں خواہشیں ایسی کہ ہر خواہش پہ دم نکلے

ہزاروں خواہشیں ایسی کہ ہر خواہش پہ دم نکلے
بہت نکلے مرے ارمان' لیکن پھر بھی کم نکلے

ڈرے کیوں میرا قاتل؟ کیا رہیگا اس کی گردن پر
وہ خوں' جو چشمِ ترسے' عمر بھر یوں دم بدم نکلے!

نکلنا خلد سے آدم کا سنتے آئے ہیں' لیکن
بہت بے آبرو ہو کر ترے کوچے سے ہم نکلے

بھرم کھل جائے' ظالم! تیرے قامت کی درازی کا
اگر اس طرہ پر پیچ و خم کا پیچ و خم نکلے

مگر لکھوائے کوئی اس کو خط تو ہم سے لکھوائے
ہوئی صبح اور گھر سے کان پر رکھ کر قلم نکلے

ہوئی اس دور میں منسوب مجھ سے بادہ آشامی
پھر آیا وہ زمانہ' جو جہاں سے جامِ جم نکلے

ہوئی جن سے توقع خستگی کی داد پانے کی
وہ ہم سے بھی زیادہ خستۂ تیغِ ستم نکلے

محبت میں نہیں ہے فرق' جینے اور مرنے کا
اسی کو دیکھ کر جیتے ہیں' جس کافر پہ دم نکلے

خدا کے واسطے پردہ نہ کعبہ کا اٹھا ظالم
کہیں ایسا نہ ہو یاں بھی وہی کافر صنم نکلے

کہاں میخانہ کا دروازہ' غالب! اور کہاں واعظ
پر اتنا جانتے ہیں' کل وہ جاتا تھا کہ ہم نکلے

95

Desires Come by the Thousands

Each desire eats up a whole life; desires come by the thousands.
I've received what I wanted many times, but still it was
 not enough.

The one who killed me should not accept blame for my death.
My life has been pouring out through my eyes for years.

In paradise, as we know, God showed Adam the door.
When I have been shown your door, I feel a shame
 deeper than his.

The tallness we all see in you is an illusion.
If somone took the tangles from your hair, we could all
 see that.

Hire me if you are commissioning a letter to her.
Every morning I come out of my house with the pen
 behind my ear.

These days people point at me and say: "This is true wine-
 drinking."
It must be time once more for Jamshid's great cup.

I am always asking others to sympathize with my pain,
But it turns out they are worse off than I am.

For devoted lovers, living and dying are about the same.
My life is sustained by looking at her but it also takes my
 life away.

For the love of God, please don't lift the curtain over the Kaaba.
Perhaps in that spot we may find an ordinary stone.

The mullah and the tavern door seem to be two separate
 things, Ghalib,
But I did notice that he was entering yesterday as I was leaving.

Part III

दुर्दे-तहे-जाम

ग़म खाने में बोदा दिले-नाकाम बहुत है
ये रंज कि कम है मए-गुलफाम बहुत है

कहते हुए साक़ी से हया आती है वर्ना
है यों कि मुझे दुर्दे-तहे-जाम बहुत है

नै तीर कमां में है, न सैयाद कमीं में
गोशे में कफ़स के मुझे आराम बहुत है

हैं अहले-ख़िरद किस रविशे-ख़ास पे नाज़ां
पा-बस्तगी-ए-रस्मो-रहे-आम बहुत है

क्या जोहद को मानूँ, कि न हो गरचे रियाई
पादाश-ए-अमल की तम-ए-खाम बहुत है

ज़मज़म ही पे छोड़ो, मुझे क्या तौफ़े-हरम से
आलूदा-बमै जामा-ए-अहराम बहुत है

है कहर कि अब भीन बने बात कि उनको
इन्कार नहीं और मुझे इबराम बहुत है

खूं होके जिगर आंख से टपका नहीं, ऐ मर्ग
रहने दे मुझे यां, कि अभी काम बहुत है

होगा कोई ऐसा भी कि 'गालिब' को न जाने
शायर तो वो अच्छा है पे बदनाम बहुत है

مجھے درد نہ جامِ بہت سے

یہ رنج کہ 'کم ہے مے گلفام' بہت ہے	غم کھانے میں بودا' دلِ ناکام بہت ہے
ہے یوں کہ مجھے دردِ نہ جام بہت ہے	کہتے ہوئے ساقی سے حیا آتی ہے' ورنہ
گوشے میں قفس کے' مجھے آرام بہت ہے	نے تیر کماں میں ہے' نہ صیاد کمیں میں
پاداشِ عمل کی طمع خام بہت ہے	کیا زہد کو مانوں کہ' نہ ہو گرچہ ریائی
پابستگیِ رسم و رہ عام بہت ہے	ہیں اہلِ خرد کس روشِ خاص پہ نازاں؟
آلودہ بے' جامۂ احرام' بہت ہے	زمزم ہی پہ چھوڑو' مجھے کیا طوفِ حرم سے؟
انکار نہیں اور مجھے اِبرام بہت ہے	ہے قہر گر اب بھی نہ بنے بات کہ' ان کو
رہنے دے مجھے یاں کہ' ابھی کام بہت ہے	خون ہو کے جگر آنکھ سے ٹپکا نہیں 'اے مرگ!

ہوگا کوئی ایسا بھی کہ' غالبؔ کو نہ جانے؟

شاعر تو وہ اچھا ہے' پہ بدنام بہت ہے

Leftovers in the Cup

For my weak heart this living in the sorrow house is more
    than enough.
The storage of rose-colored wine is also more than enough.

I'm embarrassed, otherwise I'd tell the wine-server
That even the leftovers in the cup are, for me, enough.

No arrow comes flying in; I am safe from hunters.
The comfort level I experience in this cage is more than enough.

I don't see why the so-called elite people are so proud
When the ropes of custom that tie them down are clear
    enough.

It's hard for me to distinguish sacrifice from hypocrisy,
When the greed for reward in pious actions is obvious
    enough.

Leave me alone at the Zam Zam Well; I won't circle the Kaaba.
The wine stains on my robe are alredy numerous enough.

If we can't resolve this, it will be a great injustice.
She is not unwilling and my desire is more than strong enough.

The blood of my heart has not completely exited through my
    eyes.
O death, let me stay a while, the work we have to do is
    abundant enough.

It's difficult to find a person who has no opinion about
    Ghalib.
He is a good poet, but the dark rumors about him are
    more than enough.

अब्रे बहारी का बरस कर खुलना

इश्रते-क़तरा है दरिया में फ़ना हो जाना
दर्द का हद से गुज़रना है दवा हो जाना

दिल हुआ कश्मकशे-चारा-ए-ज़हमत में तमाम
मिट गया घिसने में इस उक़्दा का वा हो जाना

ज़ोफ़ से गिरिया-ए-मुबददल ब-दमे-सर्द हुआ
बावर आया हमें पानी का हवा हो जाना

है मुझे अबरे-बहारी का बरस कर खुलना
रोते रोते ग़मे-फुर्क़त में फ़ना हो जाना

ताकि तुझपर खुले ऐजाज़े-हवा-ए-सैक़ल
देख बरसात में सब्ज़ आइने का हो जाना

बख़्शे है जल्वा-ए-गुल ज़ौक़े-तमाशा 'ग़ालिब'
चश्म को चाहिये हर रंग में वा हो जाना

ابر بہاری کا برس کر کھلنا

درد کا حد سے گزرنا ہے، دوا ہوجانا	عشرتِ قطرہ ہے، دریا میں فنا ہوجانا
مِٹ گیا، گھٹنے میں، اس عقدہ کا وا ہوجانا	دل ہوا، کش مکشِ چارۂ زحمت میں، تمام
باور آیا ہمیں پانی کا ہوا ہوجانا	ضعف سے، گریہ مُبدل بہ دمِ سرد ہوا
روتے روتے، غم فرقت میں، فنا ہوجانا	ہے مجھے، ابر بہاری کا برس کے کھلنا
دیکھ برسات میں سبز آئنہ کا ہوجانا	تاکہ تجھ پر کھلے اعجازِ ہوائے صیقل

بخشے ہے جلوۂ گل، ذوقِ تماشا، غالب!
چشم کو چاہیے ہر رنگ میں وا ہوجانا

When the Sky Clears

The drop grows happy by losing itself in the river.
A pain when beyond human range becomes something else.

One man's heart died when he insisted on treating his own
    problems.
Sometimes people solve jute-knots by rubbing them on rocks.

Since I am weak, I sigh instead of weeping.
My experience tells me that water can change and become air.

The sky abruptly clears the following thick clouds and heavy
    rain.
The clouds, recognizing separation, cried and vanished
    into nonexistence.

We make the back of the mirror green in order to see our
    faces.
Sometimes nature makes the front of the mirror green as well.

We love seeing the beauty of poppies and lilies.
When the eyes lose themselves in the colors, they are
    seeing at last.

चिराग़े-मुर्दा

सताइश गर है ज़ाहिद इस कदर जिस बाग़े-रिज़वां का
वो इक गुलदस्ता है हम बेखुदों के ताक़े-निसयां का

बयां क्या कीजिये बेदादे-काविश-हाए मिज़गां का
कि हरयक क़तरा-ए-ख़ूं दाना है तसबीहे-मरजां का

दिखाऊंगा तमाशा, दी अगर फुर्सत ज़माने ने
मेरा हर दाग़े-दिल इक तुख़्म है सर्वे-चिराग़ां का

किया आइनाख़ाने का वो नक़्शा तेरे जल्वेह ने
करे जो परतवे-ख़ुर्शीदे-आलम शबनमिस्तां का

मेरी तामीर में मुज़्मिर है इक सूरत ख़राबी की
हयूला बर्क़े-ख़िरमन का है ख़ूने-गर्म दहक़ां का

ख़मोशी में निहां ख़ूंगशता लाखों आरजूएं हैं
चिराग़े-मुर्दा हूं मैं बेज़ुबां गोरे-गरीबां का

बग़ल में गैर की आप सोए हैं कहीं वर्ना
सबब क्या ख़्वाब में आकर तबस्सुम-हाए-पिनहां का

नज़र मे हैं हमारी जादा-ए-राहे फ़ना, 'ग़ालिब'
कि ये शीराज़ा है आलम के अजज़ाए-परीशां का

چراغِ مردہ ہوں میں بے زباں گورِ غریباں کا

ستائش گر ہے زاہد اس قدر، جس باغِ رضواں کا
وہ اک گلدستہ ہے ہم بے خودوں کے طاقِ نسیاں کا

بیان کیا کیجیے بیدادِ کاوشہائے مژگاں کا
کہ ہر یک قطرۂ خوں، دانہ ہے تسبیحِ مرجاں کا

دکھاؤں گا تماشا، دی اگر فرصت زمانے نے
مراہر داغِ دل، اک تخم ہے سروِ چراغاں کا

کیا آئینہ خانے کا وہ نقشہ، تیرے جلوہ نے
کرے جوں پر تو خورشید عالم شبنستاں کا

مری تعمیر میں مضمر ہے ایک صورت خرابی کی
ہیولیٰ برقِ خرمن کا ہے خونِ گرم دہقاں کا

خموشی میں نہاں خوں گشتہ لاکھوں آرزوئیں ہیں
چراغِ مردہ ہوں، میں بے زباں گورِ غریباں کا

بغل میں غیر کی، آج آپ سوتے ہیں کہیں، ورنہ
سبب کیا خواب میں آکر تبسم ہائے پنہاں کا

نظر میں ہے ہماری، جادۂ راہِ فنا، غالب
کہ یہ شیرازہ ہے عالم کے اجزائے پریشاں کا

The Candle That Has Gone Out

Religious people are always praising the Garden of Paradise.
To us ecstatics it's a bouquet left on the bedstand of
  forgetfulness.

Her eyelashes are so sharp it's hard to describe the pain.
Each drop of eye blood is like a necklace made of coral.

If this world gives me free time, I could show you fireworks.
My heart has many scars; each scar signifies a tree all on
  fire.

You know what the reflected sunlight does to dew drops.
Your beauty has the same effect on the house of mirrors.

In my beginning there was already the essence of my end.
Lightning doesn't care about the crop, it wants the farmer.

In my silence there are thousands of blood-soaked desires.
I am like a candle that has gone out on the grave of a
  poor man.

I think you must be making love today with that man I hate.
Otherwise why should you smile so mischievously in my
  dream?

Ghalib, I think we have caught sight of the road to death now.
Death is a string that binds together the scattered beads
  of the universe.

क्या सूरतें होंगी

सब कहां? कुछ लाला-ओ-गुल में नुमायां हो गईं
ख़ाक में क्या सूरतें होंगी, कि पिनहां हो गईं

थीं बनातुलनाँश-ए-गरदूं, दिन को परदे में निहाँ
शब को उनके जी में क्या आयी कि उरियाँ हो गईं

जू-ए-ख़ूं आखों से बहने दो, कि है शामे-फ़िराक़
मैं ये समझूँगा कि शमएं दो फ़रोज़ाँ हो गईं

इन परीज़ादों से लेगें खुल्द में हम इन्तक़ाम
कुदरते-हक़ से यही हूरें अगर वाँ हो गईं

नींद उसकी है, दिमाग उसका है, रातें उसकी हैं
तेरी जुल्फ़ें जिसके बाजू पर परीशाँ हो गईं

मैं चमन में क्या गया, गोया दबिसताँ खुल गया
बुलबुलें सुनकर मेरे नाले, ग़ज़ल-ख़्वाँ हो गईं

वह निगाहें क्यों हुई जाती हैं, या रब, दिल के पार
जो मेरी कोताही-ए-किस्मत से मिज़गाँ हो गईं

वाँ गया भी मैं, तो उनकी गालियों का क्या जवाब
याद थी जितनी दुआएँ, सर्फ़े-दरबाँ हो गईं

जां फ़िज़ा है बादा जिसके हाथ में जाय आगया
सब लक़ीरें हाथ की गोया रगे जां हो गईं

हम मुवहिहद हैं, हमारा केश है तर्के-रसूम
मिल्लतें जब मिट गयीं, अजज़ा-ए-ईमाँ हो गईं

रंज से ख़ूगर हुआ इन्सान तो मिट जाता है रंज
मुश्किलें मुझ पर पड़ीं इतनी कि आसाँ हो गईं

यो ही गर रोता रहा 'ग़ालिब'तो अहले-जहाँ
देखना इन बस्तियों को तुम की वीराँ हो गईं

خاک میں کیا صورتیں ہوں گی کہ پنہاں ہو گئیں

خاک میں کیا صورتیں ہوں گی کہ پنہاں ہو گئیں
سب کہاں! کچھ لالہ و گل میں نمایاں ہو گئیں

شب کو ان کے جی میں کیا آئی کہ عریاں ہو گئیں
تھیں بناتُ النعش گردوں، دن کو پردے میں نہاں

میں یہ سمجھوں گا کہ شمعیں دو فروزاں ہو گئیں
جو یہ خوں آنکھوں سے بہنے دو کہ ہے شامِ فراق

قدرتِ حق سے یہی حوریں، اگر واں ہو گئیں
ان پری زادوں سے لیں گے خلد میں ہم انتقام

تیری زلفیں جس کے بازو پر پریشاں ہو گئیں
نیند اس کی ہے، دماغ اس کا ہے، راتیں اس کی ہیں

بلبلیں سن کر مرے نالے، غزل خواں ہو گئیں
میں چمن میں کیا گیا، گویا دبستاں کھل گیا

جو مری گوتاہی قسمت سے، مژگاں ہو گئیں
وہ نگاہیں کیوں ہوئی جاتی ہیں، یارب! دل کے پار؟

یاد تھیں جتنی دعائیں، صرف درباں ہو گئیں
واں گیا بھی میں، تو ان کی گالیوں کا کیا جواب

سب لکیریں ہاتھ کی، گویا رگِ جاں ہو گئیں
جاں فزا ہے بادہ، جس کے ہاتھ میں جام آگیا

ملتیں جب مٹ گئیں، اجزائے ایماں ہو گئیں
ہم مُوَحّد ہیں، ہمارا کیش ہے ترکِ رسوم

مشکلیں مجھ پر پڑیں اتنی کہ آساں ہو گئیں
رنج سے خوگر ہوا انساں تو مٹ جاتا ہے رنج

یوں ہی گر روتا رہا غالب، تو اے اہلِ جہاں
دیکھنا ان بستیوں کو تم کہ ویراں ہو گئیں

Where Are the Other Faces?

Only a few faces show up as roses; where are the rest?
This dust must be concealing so many poets and saints.

The Seven Pleiades hid behind a veil all day.
At night they changed their minds, and became naked.

During the night of separation red tears flow from my eyes.
I will imagine my eyes as two burning candles.

We'll seek revenge in heaven from these hard-hearted beauties.
Of course that presupposes that their destination is heaven.

That man on whose arm your hair is spread out
Owns three things: sleep, a quiet mind, and night.

When I visited the Garden, it was as if I started a school.
Even the birds gave poetry readings after hearing my cry.

O God, why do these glances of hers keep invading my heart?
What luck do I have? When I look, I see her lids.

All the good words I could remember I gave to the doorman.
How can I change her painful jibes now into blessings.

Whenever a man's hand closes around a cup of wine,
That energy-enhancer, he beleives the lines in his palm
    are life's rivers.

I beleive in one God only, and my religion is breaking rules:
When all sects go to pieces, they'll become part of the
    true religion.

When a human being becomes used to sorrow, then sorrow
    disappears;
Obstacle after obstacle fell on me, and the road was easy.

If Ghalib keeps pouring out the salt of his tears,
Dear people, I say the whole world will become a ruin.

ख़मोशी

उस बज़्म में मुझे नहीं बनती हया किये
बैठा रहा अगरचे इशारे हुआ किये

दिल ही तो है, सियासते दरबाँ से डर गया
मैं, और जाऊं दर से तेरे बिन सदा किये

रखता फिरुं हूं ख़िरक़ा-ओ-सज्जादा रहने मै
मुद्दत हुई है दावते-आबो-हवा किये

बेसफ़ा ही गुजरती है, हो गर्चे उम्रे-ख़िज़र
हज़रत भी कल कहेंगे कि हम क्या कया किये

मक़दूर हो तो ख़ाक से पूछूं कि ए लईम
तूने वो गंज-हाए-गिरांमाया क्या किये

सोहबत में ग़ैर की न पडी हो कहीं ये खू
देने लगा है बोसे बग़ैर इल्तजा किये

'ग़ालिब' तुम्ही कहो कि मिलेगा जवाब क्या
माना कि तुम कहा किये और वो सुना किये

بیٹھا رہا اگرچہ اشارے ہوا کیے

اس بزم میں' مجھے نہیں بنتی حیا کیے   بیٹھا رہا' اگرچہ اشارے ہوا کیے

دل ہی تو ہے' سیاست درباں سے ڈر گیا   میں' اور جاؤں درے سے ترے' بن صدا کیے

رکھتا پھروں ہوں' خرقہ و سجادہ رہنِ مے   مدت ہوئی ہے' دعوتِ آب و ہوا کیے

بے صرفہ ہی گزرتی ہے' ہو گرچہ عمر خضر   حضرت بھی کل کہیں گے کہ "ہم کیا کیا کیے"

مقدور ہو تو خاک سے پوچھوں کہ "اے لئیم!!"   تونے وہ گنجہائے گرا نمایہ کیا کیے؟

صحبت میں غیر کی نہ پڑی ہو یہ خو دینے لگا ہے بوسہ بغیر التجا کیے

غالبؔ! تمہیں کہو کہ ملے گا جواب کیا؟

مانا کہ تم کہا کیے اور وہ سنا کیے

117

Not Making a Commotion

When I am a guest at the Great One's party I don't feel any
    shame.
I stay there even though I pick up hints for me to go.

Ultimately it is my heart who fears the Doorkeeper.
Otherwise I would have made a commotion at the door.

I've pawned my patched robe and prayer rug to buy wine.
It's been so long since I've honored the springtime.

Each life, even the prophet Khidr's, passes by in trivialities,
On Judgement Day even Khidr will question his life.

If I had the right, I would ask Earth, "You who hide things,
What have you done with treasures buried in you?"

Let's hope she didn't pick up this habit with my rival-
She offers me kisses before I have asked for them.

What the answer to that is, you'll have to figure out, Ghalib.
We all agree that you talked a lot and they listened.

ख़स आशियाँ के लिये

नवेद-ए-अमन है बेदाद-ए-दोस्त जाँ के लिये
रही न तर्ज़े-सितम कोई आसमाँ के लिये

बला से गर मिज़ा-ए-यार तिश्ना-ए-ख़ूँ है
रखूँ कुछ अपनी भी मिज़गान-ए-ख़ूँ-फ़िशाँ के लिये

वह ज़िंदा हम हैं कि हैं रुशनास-ए-ख़ल्क, ऐ ख़िजर
न तुम, कि चोर बने उम्र-ए-जाविदाँ के लिये

रहा बला में भी मुबतिला-ए-आफ़त-ए-रश्क
बला-ए जाँ है अदा तेरी इक जहाँ के लिये

फ़लक न दूर रख उससे मुझे, कि मैं ही नहीं,
दराज़-दसती-ए-क़ातिल के इमतिहाँ के लिये

मिसाल यह मेरी कोशिश की है, कि मुर्गे-ए-असीर
करे क़फ़स में फ़राहम ख़स आशियाँ के लिये

बक़दरे-शौक़ नहीं, ज़र्फ़-ए-तंगना-ए-ग़ज़ल
कुछ और चाहिये वुसअत मेरे बयाँ के लिये

ज़बाँ पे बार-ए-ख़ुदाया, यह किसका नाम आया,
कि मेरे नुत्क़ ने बोसे मेरी ज़बाँ के लिये

ज़माना अहद में उसके है महवे-आराइश,
बनेंगे और सितारे अब आसमाँ के लिये

वरक़ तमाम हुआ और मदह बाक़ी है,
सफ़ीना चाहिये इस बहरे-बेकराँ के लिये

کرے قفس میں فراہم خس آشیاں کے لئے

نویدِ امن ہے بیدادِ دوست جاں کے لئے   رہی نہ طرزِ ستم کوئی آسماں کے لئے

بلا سے گر مژدۂ یار قصئہ خوں ہے   رکھوں کچھ اپنی بھی مژگانِ خونفشاں کے لئے

وہ زندہ ہم ہیں کہ ہیں روشناسِ خلق اے خضر   نہ تم کہ چور بنے عمرِ جاوداں کے لئے

رہا بلا میں بھی مبتلائے آفتِ رشک   بلائے جاں ہے ادا تیری اک جہاں کے لئے

فلک نہ دور رکھ اس سے مجھے، میں ہی نہیں   درازدستی قاتل کے امتحاں کے لئے

مثال یہ مری کوشش کی ہے کہ، مرغِ اسیر   کرے قفس میں فراہم خس آشیاں کے لئے

بقدرِ شوق نہیں، ظرفِ تنگ نائے غزل   کچھ اور چاہیے وسعت، مرے بیاں کے لئے

زباں پہ بارِ خدایا! یہ کس کا نام آیا؟   کہ میرے نطق نے بوسے مری زباں کے لئے

زمانہ عہد میں اس کے ہے محوِ آرائش   بنیں گے اور ستارے اب آسماں کے لئے

ورق تمام ہوا، اور مدح باقی ہے

سفینہ چاہیے اس بحرِ بے کراں کے لئے

The Bird Gathering Straws

My friend's cruel behavior is a road to happiness for me.
There is no requirement now for the heavens to be cruel.

My darling's sharp eyelashes no doubt are thirsty for blood.
But I need to save some blood for my own eyelashes that
    like to weep.

Those alive like me, O Khidr, everyone in creation knows.
To ensure your immortality you've had to hide your face
    like a thief.

I am jealous even of those people whom disaster visits.
In your style of living you bring grief to the whole creation.

O Blue Sky, let me stay close to the Great One.
Those hands that reach out and kill can be used for
    testing someone else.

The efforts I make in my life resemble a bird in a cage
Who can't stop gathering straws for her nest.

The narrow street of the ghazal actually does not fit me well.
My emotions and desires require a landscape with mountains
    and seas.

That name I want to honour so much came out of my tongue,
O God, so that even my voice started kissing my tongue.

For her crowning the whole creation is busy making gay
    decorations.
Even the sky will shortly be adding more stars.

This poem has come to an end, but my longing to praise
    hasn't.
An immense liner is required for this ocean that has no shores.

रहज़न का शुक्रिया

क़फस में हूँ गर अच्छा भी न जाने मेरे शेवन को
मेरा होना बुरा क्या है नवा-संजाने-गुलशन को

न निकला आंख से तेरी इक आंसू उस जराहत पर
किया सीने में जिसने खूंचकां मिज़गाने-सोज़न को

हुवा चर्चा जो मेरे पांव की ज़ंजीर बनने का
किया बेताब कान में जुम्बिशे-जौहर ने आहन को

वफ़ादारी, बशर्ते-उस्तुवारी असले-ईमाँ है
मरे बुतख़ाने में, तो काबे में गाड़ों बिरहमन को

शहादत थी मेरी क़िस्मत में जो दी थी ये ख़ू मुझको
जहां तलवार को देखा झुका देता था गर्दन को

न लुटता दिन को, तो कब रात को यों बेख़बर सोता
रहा खटका न चोरी का, दुआ देता हूं रहज़न को

सुख़न क्या कह नही सकते, कि जोयां हों जवाहर के
जिगर क्या हम नही रखते, कि खोदें जाके माअदन को

رہا کھٹکا نہ چوری کا، دعا دیتا ہوں رہزن کو

قفس میں ہوں، گر اچھا بھی نہ جانیں میرے شیون کو مرا ہونا برا ہے، نوا سنجانِ گلشن کو!

نہ نکلا آنکھ سے تیری اک آنسو، اس جراحت پر کیا سینے میں جس نے خوں چکاں، مژگانِ سوزن کو

ہوا چرچا جو میرے پانو کی زنجیر بننے کا کیا بے تاب کاں میں جنبشِ جوہر نے، آہن کو

وفاداری بشرطِ استواری، اصلِ ایماں ہے مرے بت خانے میں، تو کعبہ میں گاڑو برہمن کو

شہادت تھی مری قسمت میں، جو دی تھی یہ خو مجھ کو جہاں تلوار کو دیکھا، جھکا دیتا تھا گردن کو

نہ لٹتا دن کو، تو کب رات کو یوں بے خبر سوتا! رہا کھٹکا نہ چوری کا، دعا دیتا ہوں رہزن کو

سخن کیا کہہ نہیں سکتے کہ، جویاں ہوں جواہر کے؟

جگر کیا ہم نہیں رکھتے کہ، کھودیں جا کے معدن کو؟

Thanking the Robber

I agree that I'm in a cage, and I'm crying.
But my crying doesn't affect the happy birds in the garden.

The wound I have in my chest did not bring one tear from
   you.
But that wound made even the eye of the needle weep.

When people began to talk about chains for my ankles,
The gold under the ground began to twist, pushing the
   iron away.

The essence of faith is loyalty and devotion.
It's all right to bury in the Kaaba the Brahman who died
   worshiping in the temple.

My destiny was always to have my head cut off.
Whenever I see a sword, my neck bends by habit.

I can sleep well at night because I was robbed during the day.
I have to thank the robber for providing such a relaxed
   sleep.

Why should we bother about diamonds if we can write poems?
We have our own chests to dig in; why bother traveling
   to the mines?

जन्नत की बादा गुलफ़ाम व मुश्कबू

हर एक बात पे कहते हो तुम कि 'तू क्या है'
तुम्ही कहो कि ये अंदाज़े-गुफ़्तगू क्या है

न शोले में ये करिश्मा, न बर्क़ में ये अदा,
कोई बताओ कि वो शोखे-तुन्द-ख़ू क्या है

ये रश्क है, कि वो होता है हमसुख़न तुमसे
वगर ना ख़ौफ़े-बद-आमोज़िये-अदू क्या है

चिपक रहा है बदन पर लहू से पैराहन
हमारी जैब को अब हाजते-रफ़ू क्या है

जला है जिस्म जहां, दिल भी जल गया होगा
कुरेदते हो जो अब राख, जुस्तजू क्या है

रगों में दौड़ने फिरने के हम नहीं क़ायल
जब आंख से ही न टपका, तो फिर लहू क्या है

वो चीज़ जिसके लिये हमको हो बहिश्त अज़ीज़
सिवाय बादा-ए-गुलफ़ामे-मुश्कबू क्या है

पियूं शराब अगर ख़ुम भी देख लूं दो-चार
ये शीशा-ओ-क़दहो-कूज़ा-ओ-सुबू क्या है

रही न ताक़ते गुफ़्तार, और अगर हो भी
तो किस उम्मीद पे कहिये, कि आरजू क्या है

हुआ है शेह का मुसाहिब, फिरे है इतराता,
वगर ना शहर में 'ग़ालिब' की आबरू क्या है

سوائے بادۂ گلفامِ مشک بو کیا ہے

ہر ایک بات پہ کہتے ہو تم کہ "تو کیا ہے؟"   تمہیں کہو کہ یہ اندازِ گفتگو کیا ہے؟

نہ شعلہ میں یہ کرشمہ نہ برق میں یہ ادا   کوئی بتاؤ کہ، وہ شوخِ تند خو کیا ہے؟

یہ رشک ہے کہ وہ ہوتا ہے ہم سخن تم سے   وگرنہ خوفِ بد آموزیِ عدو کیا ہے؟

چیک رہا ہے بدن پر، لہو سے، پیراہن   ہماری جیب کو اب حاجتِ رفو کیا ہے؟

جلا ہے جسم جہاں، دل بھی جل گیا ہوگا!   کریدتے ہو جو اب راکھ، جستجو کیا ہے؟

رگوں میں دوڑتے پھرنے کے ہم نہیں قائل   جب آنکھ سے ہی نہ ٹپکا تو پھر لہو کیا ہے؟

وہ چیز، جس کے لیے ہم کو ہو، بہشت عزیز   سوائے بادۂ گلفامِ مشکبو کیا ہے؟

پیوں شراب، اگر خم بھی دیکھ لوں دو چار   یہ شیشہ و قدح و کوزہ و سبو کیا ہے؟

رہی نہ طاقتِ گفتار اور اگر ہو بھی   تو کس امید پہ کہیے، کہ آرزو کیا ہے؟

ہوا ہے شہ کا مصاحب، پھر ہے اتراتا

وگرنہ شہر میں غالبؔ کی آبرو کیا ہے؟

129

The Musky Wine of Heaven

Each time I open my mouth, the Great One says: "You-You,
  who are you?"
Help me, How would you describe the style of such a
  conversation?

A spark is lacking in awe. Lightning lacks playfulness.
Neither has the Great One's adroit fierceness.

My jealousy arises because my rival gets to speak to you;
Otherwise it's okay if he ruins my reputation.

Blood makes my whole shirt stick to my body.
The good thing is I don't have to repair my collar.

With the whole body cindered, the heart was clearly burnt.
Digging into the ashes, what's the point of that?

Blood flowing along through the veins doesn't impress us.
If blood doesn't drop from the eyes, it's not real blood.

My main attraction to Heaven has always been its wine-
That musky, fuschia-colored wine we've been promised.

If it's drinking time, I need large containers.
Let's put away these mingy cups and flagons.

My gift of speech is gone but even if I still had it
What reason would I have to put desire into words?

Since he's a friend of the Emperor, he oozes arrogance.
How else can Ghalib gain any respect?

पर्दे के पीछे

फिर कुछ इक दिल को बेक़रारी है
सीना जोया-ए-ज़ख़्मे-कारी है

फिर जिगर खोदने लगा नाख़ून
आमदे-फ़स्ले-लालाकारी है

क़िब्ला-ए-मक़सदे-निगाहे-नियाज़
फिर वही परदा-ए-अम्मारी है

चश्मे-दल्लाले-जिन्से-रुस्वाई
दिल ख़रीदारे-ज़ौक़े-ख़्वारी है

वही सदरंग नाला-फ़रसाई
वही सद-गुना अश्कबारी है

दिल हवाए-ख़िरामे-नाज़ से फिर
महशरिस्ताने- बेक़रारी है

जलवा फिर अर्ज़े नाज़ करता है
रोज़े-बाज़ारे-जां-सिपारी है

फिर उसी बेवफा पे मरते हैं
फिर वही ज़िंदगी हमारी है

हो रहा है जहान में अंधेर
जुल्फ़ की फिर सरिश्ता-दारी है

फिर दिया पारा-ए-जिगर ने सवाल
एक फ़रियादो-आहो-ज़ारी है

बेख़ुदी बेसबब नहीं 'ग़ालिब'
कुछ तो है जिसकी पर्दादारी है

کچھ تو ہے جس کی پردہ داری ہے

پھر کچھ اک دل کو بے قراری ہے   سینہ جویاے زخمِ کاری ہے

پھر جگر کھودنے لگا ناخن   آمد فصلِ لالہ کاری ہے

قبلۂ مقصدِ نگاہِ نیاز   پھر وہی پردۂ عماری ہے

چشم، دلالِ جنسِ رسوائی   دل، خریدارِ ذوقِ خواری ہے

وہ ہی صد رنگ نالہ فرسائی   وہ ہی صد گونہ اشک باری ہے

دل ہواے خرامِ ناز سے، پھر   محشرستانِ بے قراری ہے

جلوہ پھر عرضِ ناز کرتا ہے   روز بازارِ جاں سپاری ہے

پھر اسی بے وفا پہ مرتے ہیں   پھر وہی زندگی ہماری ہے

ہو رہا ہے جہان میں اندھیرا   زلف کی پھر سرشتہ داری ہے

پھر دیا پارۂ جگر نے سوال   ایک فریاد و آہ و زاری ہے

بے خودی بے سبب نہیں غالبؔ

کچھ تو ہے، جس کی پردہ داری ہے

Behind the Curtain

My heart is becoming restless again;
And my fingernails start looking for my chest.

My fingernails are clawing down toward my heart again.
It must be the right time for planting red tulips.

The eyes that are filled with desire have a goal-
The curtained hoodah where the elegant rider sits.

The eye's habit is to buy and sell disreputable goods.
The heart is an enthusiastic purchaser of humiliation.

I'm still giving out the same hundred colorful complaints.
Tears are falling now, but a hundred times more.

Because my heart wants so much to look at my lover's beautiful feet,
It has become a scene of great unrest like the paintings of
the Last Day.

Beauty is passing by once more and showing her style
So we know that someone will shortly die in the public square.

We die over and over for the same unfaithful person.
Our life has fallen back into the old familiar ways.

The whole world is sinking into darkness and corruption
Because she has just thrown back her beautiful hair.

Once more the mashed pieces of the heart send in their
petitions
Asking why the pain in this world is so repetitive.

The amount of ecstasy has to make some sense, Ghalib.
There must be something hiding behind the curtain.

ज़ख्मे तेग़

कहूं जो हाल, तो कहते हो 'मुद्आ कहिये'
तुम्हीं कहो, कि जो तुम यों कहो, तो क्या कहिये

न कहियो ताअन से फिर तुम, कि 'हम सितमगर हैं'
मुझे तो ख़ू है कि जो कुछ कहो, बजा कहिये

वो नश्तर सही, पर दिल में जब उतर जाये
निगाहे-नाज़ को फिर क्यों न आश्ना कहिये

नहीं ज़रीआ-ए-राहत, जराहत-ए-पैकां
वह ज़ख़्म-ए-तेग है, जिसको कि दिल-कुशा कहिये

रहे न जान, तो क़ातिल को ख़ूं-बहा दीजे
कटे ज़बान तो ख़ंजर को मरहबा कहिये

नहीं निगार को उल्फत, न हो, निगार तो है
रवानी-ए-रविश-ओ-मस्ती-ए-अदा कहिये

नहीं बहार को फुर्सत, न हो, बहार तो है
तरावते-चमन-ओ-ख़ूबी-ए-हवा कहिये

सफ़ीना जबकि किनारे पे आ लगा 'ग़ालिब'
ख़ुदा से क्या सितम-ओ-जोरे नाख़ुदा कहिये

وہ زخمِ تیغ ہے جس کو کہ دل کشا کہیے

کہوں جو حال' تو کہتے ہو: "مدعا کہیے"   تمہیں کہو کہ 'جو تم یوں کہو' تو کیا کہیے

نہ کہیو طعن سے پھر تم کہ "ہم ستم گر ہیں"   مجھے تو خوں ہے کہ 'جو کچھ کہو' بجا کہیے

وہ نیشتر سہی' پر دل میں جب اتر جاوے   نگاہِ ناز کو پھر کیوں نہ آشنا کہیے؟

نہیں ذریعہ راحت' جراحتِ پیکاں   وہ زخمِ تیغ ہے' جس کو کہ دل کشا کہیے

رہے نہ جان تو قاتل کو خوں بہا دیجے   کٹے زباں تو خنجر کو مرحبا کہیے

نہیں نگار کو الفت' نہ ہو' نگار تو ہے   روانیِ روش و مستیِ ادا کہیے

نہیں بہار کو فرصت' نہ ہو' بہار تو ہے   طراوتِ چمن و خوبیِ ہوا کہیے

سفینہ جب کہ کنارے پہ آ لگا غالبؔ!
خدا سے کیا ستم و جورِ ناخدا کہیے؟

137

The Sword Wound

When I describe my condtion, you say, "What's your point?"
When you talk to me that way, what am I to say?

Please don't mention again-even in jest-that you torture people.
My problem is that I agree too much with everything you
    say.

One of her glances works like a sharp knife.
We consider it an act of friendship because the knife-edge
    doesn't enter the heart.

To me the wound an arrow makes is insufficient.
Some people call a sword wound the opener of the heart.

When I am dead, give the killer a reward for my death.
If my tongue gets cut off, send the gift to the knife.

Your lover may not be faithful, but she is your lover.
We could mention the beautiful rolling wey she walks.

Spring doesn't last long but at least it *is* spring.
It would be good to mention the scented winds that
    move through the garden.

Ghalib, once the boat has arrived at the other shore,
Why go on and on about the wickedness of the boatman?

Ghalib and His Work

The Ghazal

All the poems in this book belong to the poetic form called the ghazal. The word "ghazal" means, literally, a conversation with the beloved. Thus the ghazal is essentially a love poem; the beloved can be a human being or God. The ghazal form originated in Iran, probably around the tenth century, and arrived in India in the twelfth century. We could call the period between the eighteenth and nineteenth centuries the golden period for this poetic form in the Urdu language. Poetic forms in Urdu include *qusidas,* poems about battles that usually praise a king or patron; or *nazms,* in which the poet sticks to a single theme; or *rubais,* which are brief poems of four lines. In the Urdu tradition, however, the ghazal remains the most popular form.

The ghazal is a complicated poetic form with a number of requirements. One is the *radif,* which is the name given to a single word repeated in a set pattern throughout the poem. Such a word—perhaps "be" or "can" or "do"—will end both lines of the first sh*er,* or couplet, in the poem. This word then reappears, ending the second line of all succeeding couplets. In the poem here called "Leftovers in the Cup," which opens Part III, we have followed this scheme so that the reader can see how the *radif* scheme shows itself.

Another requirement is the *kafiya* complication: all the words immediately preceding the *radif*—wherever it appears—must rhyme with each other. The *kafiya* rhyme, for example, might include "nazar," "par," "bhar," and so on. This we have not attempted. Generally, our translations aim to present clearly the poet's meaning and to be true to the image and surprising turns of the thought in the poems. The amazing intensity of Ghalib's feeling has been our emphasis.

As we have mentioned, the ghazal is made up of couplets called *shers*. A *sher* is a highly condensed poem of two lines and can stand on its own as an individual poem; a good *sher* is detachable and independently quotable. One *sher* might be in essence a tiny love poem; the next might contain a philosophical idea; the next might be a sally against intellectuals; the next might be an intimate confession. In a ghazal, no clear theme binds one *sher* to the next. In size, a ghazal usually consists of five to fifteen *shers*. Traditionally, the last *sher* contains the pen name of the poet and is more personal in tone.

A common meter in each ghazal is a further requirement. The Urdu meter depends on varying length of sound rather than on stress as in English.

Life and Family

Ghalib was born in Agra on December 27, 1797, as Mirza Asadullah Beg Khan. In the tradition of Urdu poets, he adopted a pen name, Ghalib, which means "victorious." Ghalib was born when the power of the Mughal Empire was fading, and India was being governed more and more by the British colonials. Resistance to the British was already building up, and Delhi experienced considerable turmoil during the poet's lifetime. Ghalib was said to have witnessed over twenty thousand hangings by the British following the first major rebellion against the British in 1857. He also suffered when the British recaptured Delhi from the rebels and retaliated in part by destroying the personal libraries of his two friends, Nawab Ziaudin Khan and Nawab Husain Mirza, who kept the only copies of Ghalib's poems. Ghalib mentions in a letter that one poem was recovered when a beggar came to the door and recited a Ghalib poem as a way of requesting food.

Ghalib was from a family of Turkish aristocrats that had migrated to India to seek better fortune. Ghalib's father died in a battle when the poet was four years old; his mother, brother, and sister then moved in with their uncle on the mother's side. The maternal side of Ghalib's family was very wealthy, and he was provided an education proper for the sons of aristocratic Muslim families. Dependence on the maternal family in India was (and still is) considered deeply humiliating. Perhaps this accounts for Ghalib's lifelong search for security and a regular income. In his poems, it appears that he lived with a sense that many people regarded him as inferior.

During the early years of his life, Ghalib was helped financially by his mother, his wife's family, and several patrons. (Ghalib was married into a high-ranking family when he was thirteen; he and his wife had children, but they all died in infancy.) The government also gave him, on and off, a pension related to his father's services. However, his constant indulgences in wine and gambling usually left him heavily in debt.

Ghalib learned Persian during his early life, and he himself remarks that he was composing poetry in Persian by the time he was eleven. He was also writing poetry in Urdu, and some of the greatest poems in this book were composed before he reached the age of seventeen. Ghalib was already a well-known poet and public figure when he moved to Delhi, where the family of his wife lived, in 1810. His friends in Delhi included most of the distinguished literary people of the time.

Despite that, he was not at first accepted at court. The Emperor of Delhi, Bahadur Shah Zafar, was himself a poet, but had appointed as his poetry advisor a poet named Zauq who clearly disliked both Ghalib's poetry and his way of life. Ghalib, for his part, did not like the Emperor's poetry and often made fun of Zauq. His poem "The Musky Wine of Heaven" contains some mockery of Zauq in the last stanza: "Since he's a friend of the Emperor, he oozes arrogance." Apparently Zauq reported this to the Emperor, and when Ghalib was brought before him, the Emperor said, "I hear you have a new ghazal." Ghalib recited the ghazal from memory, ingeniously rewriting the last line on the spot so it became: "But how else can Ghalib gain any respect?" In this way he held himself up for ridicule as well.

By the time Zauq died, Ghalib had become one of the most famous poets in India. The Emperor then had no choice but to select Ghalib to replace *Zauq*.

Ghalib lived to be seventy-two years old. Out of the 235 ghazals in Urdu with which he was satisfied, we have chosen 30 for this collection.

Tales about Ghalib

There is hardly a subject that Ghalib did not write about in a spirited way, making him one of the most quoted Urdu poets. I remember the elders of my family reciting a couplet of his to add pungency to a given occasion, perhaps a family disagreement or a marriage or a funeral. Even members of Parliament in India often recite a Ghalib couplet to sum up a situation or their point of view.

Ghalib is most famous for his Urdu poetry, though he wrote many poems in Persian. Even in his Urdu poetry, Ghalib used many Persian words and constructions. His style was felt to be elegant but difficult right from the start—original though incomprehensible to most people. For that obscurity, he took heavy criticism. He defended himself from his critics in one poem:

I agree, O heart, that my ghazals are not easy to take in.
When they hear my work, experienced poets

Tell me I should write something easier to understand.
I have to write what's difficult, otherwise it is difficult
    to write.

In the early years Ghalib rejected all criticism, but a close friend, Fazl i Haq, urged him to stop writing solely in such a complex and unintelligible mode. Ghalib listened. He kept his original turns of thought but learned to shape his poetry to make it more accessible. Later, when he was compiling his Urdu poetry for a collected edition, he decided that two-thirds of his poems were not good enough to be included.

Ghalib was a Muslim, but at the same time a freethinker, tolerant of all other religions, and he had friends among Hindus as well as Muslims. His irreverent humor shows in his poetry, along with his spiritual intensity.

He did not believe in the renunciation of sensuous enjoyments. One day, walking with the Emperor and his family in the orchard, Ghalib was admiring the mangoes. The Emperor asked, "What are you looking at?"

Ghalib remarked, "Our tradition says that each grain of cereal has the name written on it of the person who will eat it. I am looking to see if my name is written on any of these mangoes."

His spontaneity is evident in another well-known story still told about him. Colonel Burns,, who had been appointed the British military governor of Delhi following the Sepoy Mutiny against the British, summoned all the aristocrats to determine who might have favored the rebels. Most people he called in felt the danger and spoke very carefully. Ghalib, however, appeared as usual in flamboyant clothes and a conical hat. The colonel asked, "Are you a Muslim or a Hindu?"

"I am a half-Muslim."

The colonel was amused. "How can that be?"

"Sir, I don't eat pork, but I do drink."

Burns responded to the wit and bravery by excusing Ghalib from any further questioning.

Ghalib makes clear in many of his poems that he was fond of wine; he was also fond of gambling and the company of courtesans. Sufi poets, when they use the words "wine" and "the tavern," mean the state of the soul, but when Ghalib uses these words, he means wine and taverns.

Although Urdu poetry had a tradition called *Ustad-Shagird,* roughly translatable as a mentor/master-apprentice tradition, no *Ustad* or master guided Ghalib's poetic talents. Ghalib himself did, however, mentor several students, training them in Urdu writing.

Ghalib's Place Among Poets

Though Ghalib is considered the best Urdu *Shair*—that is, writer of the ghazals—of all time, his poetry has not been as widely recognized in the West as has the work of many other poets who wrote in Persian, such as Rumi and Hafiz. Omar Khayyam, who has a modest ability in comparison to Ghalib, has become very well known in the West. One could say that in thought and intellect, Ghalib resembles Rumi and Hafiz, but the emotion of his poems goes in a different direction from the Sufis. Ghalib has great spiritual intensity, but it comes with a worldliness of the sort we associate with Shakespeare more than with Wordsworth or Herbert.

The capacity of Urdu for holding ambiguous meanings makes translation of Ghalib into English, essentially a language of clarity, particularly difficult. Urdu is a superb language for expressing emotion and subtlety. Urdu draws many words from the medieval languages of India, but it is also deeply influenced by Persian. It has absorbed many Persian words and continues to be written in Persian script. In Urdu, words convey subtle shades of meaning, so that a well-composed couplet will shine, so to speak, with several colors at once. One constantly finds hidden meanings in a *sher* that seemed straightforward on first reading. Such ambiguity of the original *sher* is apparent in the following two lines from 'The Bird Gathering Straws":

मिसाल यह मेरी कोशिश की है कि मुर्ग-ए-असीर
करे कफस में फराहम खस आशियाँ के लिये

Basically the couplet says that the struggles of Ghalib's life resemble the constant effort of a captive bird to collect twigs for a nest. The original Urdu allows us to contemplate at the same time three different interpretations without really tilting toward any one of the three. First, the bird has refused to accept the truth and is indulging itself. Second, the bird is following its nesting instinct even in captivity. Third, the bird knows very well that it is a captive and has no hope of freedom, but has *therefore* decided to make a nest. Urdu, in its rhythm, musicality, and expressiveness, offers an endlessly intriguing abundance. Even in translation, some of the resonance of the original suggests itself through the startling shift of mood from one *sher* to the next.

Earlier Translations

Ours is not the first attempt to translate Ghalib. In the bibliography, we mention several earlier attempts. Some poems put into English by Hindi and Urdu speakers include highly archaic English words, and Ghalib's freshness is lost.

In 1962, the Indian poet Aijaz Ahmad embarked on an admirable attempt to bring Ghalib into English with the help of a number of American poets. Each poet was given a literal version prepared by scholars and encouraged to write what he or she chose, even if it was an embroidery on the original. Some poems came through. But Ghalib's emotional world, his loneliness and sense of failure, was so far from the optimistic mood of American poetry that the translators unwittingly drew more reassuring images from the text than Ghalib intended. For this book, the collaborators returned again and again to the Urdu text. We know that no translation can ever equal the subtlety of the original poem, but I have been impressed by Robert's ability to convey very complex ideas, and still preserve much of the original beauty.

—Sunil Dutta

Selected Bibliography

Ahmad, A, Ed., *Ghazals of Ghalib: Versions from Urdu*. New York: Oxford University Press, 1994.

Husain, Y., *Urdu Ghazals of Ghalib*. New Delhi: Ghalib Institute Publishing, 1977.

Newborn, S., *Ghazals of Ghalib*. Santa Barbara, CA: Bandanna Books, 1996.

Russell, R., and Islam, K., *Ghalib: Life and Letters*. New York: Oxford University Press, 1994.

About the Editors

Robert Bly is the author, editor, and translator of numerous works of poetry and prose. His books include the most recent *Eating the Honey of Words: New and Selected Poems, Morning Poems, The Soul Is Here for Its Own Joy: Sacred Poems from Many Cultures,* published by The Ecco Press, and *Meditations on the Insatiable Soul* as well as *Iron John, The Sibling Society,* and *The Maiden King,* which he wrote with Marion Woodman. Robert Bly lives in Minnesota.

    Sunil Dutta is a biologist as well as a student of classical Indian music and literature. He is helping to preserve the ancient musical tradition called Dhrupad in India. He was born in Jaipur, India, and now lives in Los Angeles, California.